This book is dedicated to my wife and sons.

ABOUT THE AUTHOR

Sam Kohl is president of the New York School of Dog Grooming, the world's oldest and largest school of dog grooming, established in 1960. He has been active in all phases of the pet industry since 1949 when he owned his first pet shop, Guppy & Puppy. Mr. Kohl has also authored three other books:

The All Breed Dog Grooming Guide
Boarding Kennel Management
Your Career in Animal Services

I am deeply indebted to Anne Palmer for her advice and the wonderful line drawings in this book. Without these drawings, this project would have been half the fun it was.

My gratitude to Ann Sergi of the American Kennel Club Library for her kind and valuable assistance through the years. A special thanks also to her entire staff for their help with this book.

Special thanks, to my friends Chet Collier and Rita Lynch of the Westminster Kennel Club for their help and the information about the Westminster Kennel Club and the Westminster Dog Show contained herein.

Finally, *thanks* to Sam Radmin for his patience, and allowing me to make changes after everytime I said that this book was ready to be printed.

ALL ABOUT DOG SHOWS

BY SAM KOHL

Table of Contents

"Hope the judge doesn't think my puppy is too fat!"

INTRODUCTION

If you love dogs, you owe it to yourself to go to a dog show now and then. You will see hundreds of beautiful dogs. You will find that their owners are delighted to answer your questions. If you stay at ringside long enough to see a complete judging from beginning to end, chances are high that you'll get caught up in the excitement and end up cheering and clapping for the successful competitors along with your fellow dog fanciers.

This book is an attempt to explain dog shows to the newcomer to the dog fancy. We want to help you feel at home at the shows. We want to show you that dog shows are not as complicated as they're cracked up to be, that "dog people" are neither clannish nor crazy, and that the sport of showing dogs is one of the most sociable and satisfying hobbies that you could hope to find.

We will mainly be discussing the type of dog show known as the "conformation show." This is the type of show in which dogs are judged on points of structure and how well they conform to the breed standard. In other words, they are judged for what they are, rather than for what they do. Dogs are also judged for what they do in obedience trials, which we will explain briefly later in the text.

Even if you have no intention of ever entering a dog in a show, this book is written for you. We want to help newcomers to understand—and, most of all, *enjoy*— what they are seeing when they attend a dog show as spectators or as potential participants.

"What is a dog show anyway?"

2

CHAPTER 1

WHAT? YOU'VE NEVER BEEN TO A DOG SHOW?

If you've never been to a real dog show, take heart, you're not alone. Although the ranks of dog show spectators have grown enormously and quickly over the last few years, there are still thousands of dog enthusiasts around the world who, for one reason or another, have never attended a show, or have attended only one or two, even though they would really like to join the fun.

Come On In!

It's easy to join the ranks of the show world. Hundreds and hundreds of shows are held—usually on Saturdays or Sundays—in the United States every year. No matter where you live, there will soon be a show near you. To find out when and where these local shows will be held, check the latest issue of *Purebred Dogs*, the *American Kennel Club Gazette* or *Dog World* magazine. The sports section of many larger newspapers is another place to look for dog show announcements.

Attending a Dog Show

So you've seen an advertisement or heard that there is to be a dog show nearby, and you've decided to attend. What can you reasonably hope to gain from attending this show? Mainly, we would hope, you will gain pleasure. Dog shows are great fun, and anyone who loves dogs will almost certainly enjoy the experience of spending a day watching beautiful, perfectly groomed, well-behaved dogs go through their paces in the ring.

There are, however, other reasons for going to a show. You might, for example, be considering acquiring a new dog. If that's the situation, then a dog show is a fine place to become familiar with the different breeds that you have to choose from. Do you want a tiny dog to keep you company in your small apartment? Then look around the show grounds for the toy breeds. You will see the active, agile, little Pomeranians and Chihuahuas, the elegant and sophisticated Italian Greyhounds, and the fairy-like white Maltese, as well as many other small breeds.

Should you be in the market for a dog to accompany you when hunting for game, search out the sporting dogs. You will see various pointers, setters and spaniels at any all-breed show.

Indeed, looking for a puppy or a new dog of any age at a dog show is a wise move. Many of the exhibitors present are dog breeders of record. Since their own dogs are of show quality, you have an excellent chance of finding a superior quality, perfectly healthy pet at a show.

On the other hand, perhaps you already have your own pure-bred dog and are interested in mating it with another really fine dog. Where else but a dog show to go shopping for a mate worthy of your pet?

You may go to a dog show, then, for any or all of these reasons, or you may go for the sheer fun of it. You have no idea of what to expect since you don't know what will really be going on, but you are willing to give this sport a try.

Indoor and Outdoor Dog Shows

Depending upon the time of year and the location of the show, the event may take place either at an indoor arena or on an outdoor field. It is important to dress accordingly for comfort. When attending an indoor show, you can be reasonably certain that the arena—often an armory or large gymnasium—will be heated and quite comfortable, but take a sweater with you anyway, as those wide open arenas can be very drafty.

At an outdoor show there will usually be a tent set up in case of rain, for the show will go on in spite of bad weather. Don't count on being able to take refuge in the tent, however, because it will get crowded very fast—as soon as the first falling raindrop hits the field! You should be prepared for any sudden weather changes that might occur while you're at an outdoor show. A light raincoat and an umbrella should be part of your equipment if there is any chance of rain. Equally important are sunglasses, a wide-brimmed hat, and a light, long-sleeved shirt on days when the sun threatens to blister and blind you. Indoors or out, you will need comfortable, flat-heeled shoes because you will be walking or standing most of the time.

At outdoor shows, in addition to the proper clothing, you might want to take a light, folding stool since there is rarely adequate seating available. Don't take your favorite reclining beach chair, though as it will probably take up too much room at ringside.

Sometimes one hair style resembles another.

CHAPTER 2

WHAT IS A DOG SHOW ANYWAY?

Many people think that a dog show is an event at which dog owners just parade their pets around a ring to the admiration of other proud pet owners. There's certainly no harm in viewing a show this way. You probably suspect, however, that the whole thing is a bit more complicated than that, and if so, you are right.

Keep in mind that there are different kinds of dog shows. In the biggest city or in the tiniest farm community, there are certain to be some dog fanciers around. These fanciers, once they find one another—and they *always* find one another eventually— band together and form kennel clubs. The kennel clubs then sponsor dog shows.

Let's consider these types of shows one at a time. The best known shows are the "biggies," of course. Santa Barbara, California, for example, was the site of a dog show which, in a recent year, drew more than 4,300 entries. The shows held annually in Dallas, Texas and San Jose, California, usually come close to 3,000 entries apiece. Some of these very large shows are held in sports centers with massive exhibition areas. The atmosphere is festive, with refreshment stands, balloons, and parking space for thousands of cars. Some shows even have closed circuit television systems so that you can watch the poodle judging on a TV screen while you wait in line for coffee and a hot dog at the other end of the building. These giant shows, whether they're held inside a great sports complex or outside on a grassy field, are great fun for local families who own pet dogs as well as for show dog exhibitors.

The big city, high prestige shows such as the rapidly growing International in Chicago and the Westminster in New York, assume a slightly different character. At these big city shows, although they do not always have the highest number of entries, you will see many of the finest dogs in the United States. The shows may be noisy and crowded; parking may be difficult; hotel accommodations may be dreadful; food inedible; weather cruel; pressure unbearable. There are no festive balloons, no colorful tents and no children in strollers. But these are *the* shows to enter. And to win at International or Westminster is the greatest honor that can be bestowed on a dog and his owner.

Every February at Westminster, one hears the same complaints: dreadful hotels, no free parking, crowded grooming area, ghastly food, congested benching area, beastly weather. But every February they return to battle the crowds and the weather, to complain, and maybe—just maybe—to win. Even to be entered at Westminster is an honor for no dog is accepted unless he has already won points at another show. But to win at this show is every exhibitor's dream—whether he admits it or not.

Very small shows held in less populous areas of this country may lack the press coverage given to Westminster and the colorful show grounds of the larger shows, but the spirit will be there just the same. At the Kenai Kennel Club show in Alaska in a recent year there were 277 dogs entered. That's a far cry from the 2,777-dog entry at San Jose, California, that same year, but these little shows have great advantages. At a small show, the spectator gets to see every judging. He doesn't have to choose between watching the Afghans or the Pekingese because the two breeds are being judged simultaneously in two different rings. Also, at a small show, people have a chance to talk to one another. A visitor is free to ask questions of the exhibitors and breeders who are not frantically running about to get to their faraway rings in time for their judgings.

Specialty shows are those shows in which only one breed is entered. Usually small in size, the "spec" is a fine place to learn about a certain breed. A person who has been thinking about getting a Doberman, for example, might do well to find a Doberman specialty at which he can compare many good Dobermans, choose the type he most admires, and speak to the owner on the spot.

Another type of dog show is the obedience trial, which we will discuss at some length later on. As its name implies, this show is one at which the dog is judged on his brains rather than his beauty. Obedience trials are friendly, relaxed affairs. Here you will find owners who are enormously proud of their dogs and more than willing to tell you anything you want to know.

Match shows are the most casual of all dog events. They are practice shows, actually, at which prizes may be awarded but not points. Matches give inexperienced handlers a chance to practice with their dogs in a show situation. It is at a match show that a dog owner "gets the feel" of working with his dogs in a ring. For the spectator, a match show is a fine opportunity to learn show procedure.

At the mention of so many different types of shows, you might be ready to throw your hands up in confusion. But you shouldn't get discouraged, as the show world is actually not that bewildering. A dog show is, to put it quite simply, a canine beauty pageant in which prizes are awarded in points, ribbons, and silver trophies instead of rhinestone tiaras. It's rather like having many Miss America contests for our four-legged friends going on in many towns all year round. Instead of parading up and down a boardwalk, the dogs parade around a ring; instead of resting with a panel of judges, the final decision rests with one person; and instead of having two beautiful legs, the winner will have twice as many.

Anne Palmer.

1978.

Examining a dog's bite demands intense scrutiny,
WITH NO FEAR OF HARM.

CHAPTER 3

SHOW DOGS ARE VERY DIFFERENT

All of us see a lot of dogs throughout an average day. They can be seen strolling in the streets, shopping with their masters in stores, selling products in television commercials, and staring at us from car windows as we wait for the light to turn green. Dogs are one of the largest businesses in America today. They're everywhere! How are *show* dogs different from our own dogs and those of our neighbors?

Show dogs are bred, trained, groomed and handled to dazzle the judge and the spectators. One of the purposes of shows is to improve the quality of the various breeds. When a litter is born—after a very careful selection of breeding partners—the breeder of the litter watches the puppies to see which ones develop into the best examples of the breed. As they grow, the breeder might notice that Chubby, sweet and loving as he is, has flop ears when he should have ears that stand up perfectly straight. Chubby will make a fine pet, but he will not be shown because the breeder knows that he will not win. A week or so later, the breeder finds that stout-hearted little Fuzzy has developed several patches of white on her back. In a breed that is supposed to be a solid color, this is a disqualification. Fuzzy is out of the running. Little Chappie is picture-perfect, a glorious example of what a show specimen should be. But Chappie is feisty and independent, and snaps at strangers who try to touch him. When a stranger touches his master, Chappie growls and threatens to bite. This will never do! Show

♪♪
Hairy tails it is true,
Are quite easy to do,
From the very start.
It's not harder you'll find,
To be gentle and kind,
'til the grooming's through. ♪♪

12

dogs must tolerate being touched and examined, and they cannot be overprotective of their masters. The breeder *might* be able to train Chappie out of his bad qualities and turn him into a show dog. If he can't, then the breeder must turn to his remaining puppy, Holly. Holly has the required docile temperament, keen intelligence and tractability, solid black coat, straight ears, fine bone structure, good teeth and perfect health. She will be more than a pet: she will be a star.

As a show dog, Holly might live in a kennel so that she will become accustomed to the company of other dogs. In the kennel she cannot be run over by a car or stolen by a "dognapper." She will learn to work with kennel assistants as well as with her beloved master. She will be outdoors much of the time but will have a heated room at one end of the run. She will not have to depend on someone to walk her for exercise because she can run as much as she likes in her own fenced enclosure.

Being a show dog does not mean that the dog *has* to live in a kennel, though. Maybe Holly's breeder will make her a house pet. As long as he doesn't let her get impossibly spoiled, and as long as he sees that she gets enough exercise and training, there is no reason why she can't be both a star and a pet.

Whether she lives in the house or in a kennel, Holly will spend much of the first year of her life in preparation for her show career. She will be groomed and trained daily. She will be introduced to strangers very often. She will rehearse her part over and over until the big day comes when she makes her debut at her first point show. Point shows are held by those all-breed or specialty clubs that are sanctioned by the AKC to award points toward the championship title—these shows are the major league of dog competition.

"I think there's a chance we'll get looked at today."

CHAPTER 4

THE MAKING OF A DOG SHOW

A successful dog show involves the combined efforts of many different people. Not only dog owners are involved; kennel club members, superintendents and their crews, judges, stewards, handlers, exhibitors, photographers, and pet product salesmen are also included.

The whole affair begins when a local kennel club, deciding that it wants to sponsor a dog show, obtains permission to do so from the American Kennel Club. The AKC has the authority to approve the date on which the show is to be held, the classes which will be held, the prizes that will be awarded, the judges who will officiate, and the location where the event will take place.

The Superintendent

Early in the planning of a dog show, a superintendent makes his appearance on the scene. Licensed by the AKC, the superintendent will work closely with the sponsoring club to ensure that the whole event runs smoothly. It is the superintendent who will provide tents, ring enclosures, folding chairs, litter baskets, signs, and other paraphernalia for the show. The crew will arrive hours before show time in a fleet of trucks, if it is to be a big show. They will set up the grounds according to the wishes of the sponsoring club. If changes must be made during the show, then the superintendent's men will combine two rings into one, set up extra rings, take down all small ring enclosures, rearrange the field into one big ring, and otherwise see to it that the physical set-up is exactly what the sponsoring club wants it to be. When the show is over, it is the superintendent who sees to it that every trace of the show, including the trash, is removed so that the grounds look exactly as they did before the show was held.

The Premium List

Another of the superintendent's responsibilities is the printing of the premium list. This list is the official announcement sent out to owners of show dogs several weeks before the event is actually to take place, A dog owner or handler sits down with the premium list when it arrives and studies it carefully, for it will contain all of the vital information about the show. Among the facts to be found in a typical premium list are the following:

* Date, time, and location of the show
* Name of sponsoring club
* Benching information
* Parking, camping, refreshment, and hotel information
* Directions to the show grounds by car
* Names of officers of sponsoring club
* Name and address of superintendent
* Breeds and classes to be judged
* Trophies and special prizes offered
* Entry blanks to be filled out by exhibitors
* Names of veterinarians in charge
* Names of judges and their breed assignments

It is the responsibility of the superintendent to see that this premium list is mailed to dog owners well in advance of the show.

The Judge

The last item given in the above list is of extreme importance to exhibitors. People who show their dogs observe the different judges at work in many different shows. They come to know which judges like their dogs and which judges do not. Exhibitors then spread the word among their fellow show-dog owners. Their comments to one another might sound something like this:

"Judge Drayton never puts up (chooses as winner) a beagle with a very long tail. You might as well keep Yipper at home next month."

"Judge Greyling loves Newfoundlands with strong necks. Why not enter Bounder under him in the Midvale show?"

"Be sure to enter Nanny at Center City. Harriett Bobsno is judging, and she loves a thick, honey colored coat like Nanny's."

It is in this way that judges acquire their reputations among exhibitors, and an exhibitor often decides to enter a particular show because the breed judge whose name appears in the premium list is one who is known to like the type of dog he owns.

The reverse is also true sometimes. Let's give an example: Exhibitor Shirley Garvey has, let's say, a splendid black and white (harlequin) Great Dane that she believes is capable of going to championship and beyond. Judge Farswell D. Blodgett, who will judge Danes at the next show, is known to award points only to fawn-colored Danes and never to harlequins. Shirley knows that she would be wasting her time and money by showing under Judge Blodgett. She passes over this show and enters another, maybe next weekend, in which the Dane judge is known to prefer harlequins.

We will hear more about judges later. Since they are among the most important figures at any dog show, they will be treated in a section of their own when the time comes.

The Show Catalog

The show catalog, available at all dog shows, serves as a reference tool for spectators and exhibitors. Each dog entered

"Don't they KNOW this should be called a DOGALOG and not a catalog?"

at a show is designated by a number which his handler wears on an armband while the dog is being shown. No names of dogs or owners are used in the ring. If you want to know a dog's name, or the name of his owner, breeder, or handler, you must look up his number in the catalog.

Suppose that you have always wanted a fawn Pekingese and have gone to this show to find a breeder from whom you can buy one. In the ring you see the dog of your dreams— Number 34. Look up that number under "Pekingese" in your catalog. You will find the names of the dog, his sire and dam (father and mother), his owner, breeder, and handler. You will also find his date of birth. The names and addresses of the owners are listed in the back of the catalog so that you may write to them later if you don't get a chance to speak to them during the show.

Do try to talk with the owner at the show, though. There is no need to feel shy about going up to an owner and asking questions about his or her dog. Most owners, especially if they are also breeders, love to talk about their breed.

If the owner doesn't want to part with that dream Pekingese that you saw in the ring, then perhaps he can direct you to another breeder who has a similar dog for sale. Remember that show-quality dogs go for premium prices.

The show catalog is a gold mine of information about this show and about dog shows in general, and you will certainly want to invest in a copy as soon as you arrive at the show grounds. Catalogs are usually sold at a booth situated in a prominent place, often near the entrance. If you don't see the catalog booth right away, just stop any show visitor you see carrying a catalog and ask him where he got it. Dog show people are generally very helpful and will gladly point you to the catalog table.

BEST
OF
BREED

Anne Palmer.   1977.

Sometimes a handler dresses—to suit the particular occasion.

BEST
OF
BREED

"Showbiz can really be a bore at times."

CHAPTER 5

NOW THAT YOU'RE HERE...

Let's say that you saw a dog show announcement in your local newspaper. You made a note of the date and the location and have arrived early in the morning and purchased your catalog. Right now you are standing in the middle of an enormous sports arena, and you are surrounded by tumult and chaos. Dogs are everywhere—underfoot, on leashes, in cages or pens, barking and playing and leaping and whining and cavorting and generally carrying on. Men from the superintendent's crew are scurrying about with carts and brooms, crates and loudspeakers. Everyone seems to know everyone else, and—worse yet—everyone seems to know exactly what's going on...except you!

What should you do? Relax! Walk around and get your bearings. If you see someone who's not busy, speak to her or him. Ask a question. Tell her how beautiful her dog is. Smile.

The Benching Area

If this is the type of show known as a "benched" show, there will be a large area with rows of benches near where the dogs are to be exhibited. This would be a good place to begin your visit. Here the dogs are grouped by breed. Why not choose your favorite breed to visit first? But your favorites are the Irish Setters, you say, and you can't find them! Solve that problem the easy way, ask someone where the Irish Setters are. As you work your way toward those beautiful setters, take note of the hundred or more other breeds you pass along the way.

If you love dogs, you will find a stroll through the benching area delightful. When you see an animal you particularly like, why not look him up in that catalog of yours and find out what his name is? The name in the catalog will be his official name, the one under which he is registered with the AKC. It might be, for instance, Throgmorton's Foggybottom of Thunder Hill, or Judy-Mae's Peppermint Cupcake Cutie Pie. But dogs are almost never called by their official names. If the dog handler or owner is nearby, ask what the dog's *call name* is. He's probably called "Thunder" and she's probably called "Cupcake" by friends. The dogs in the benching area are so beautiful that you will want to reach out and pet them. Resist the temptation unless the owner invites you to touch the dogs. You should also avoid exciting the dogs by calling to them, feeding them, or trying to play with them. These dogs need to be kept as calm and serene as possible if they are to win when they go into the ring.

Not all shows are benched, so you might not be able to wander through such a delightful area at every show you attend. Benched shows are not very common nowadays, however, so if there is no benching area at the show you attend, why not try the next best thing—the grooming area?

The Grooming Area

At an outdoor show, the grooming area is usually under a tent. Indoors, this area is often at one end of the arena. You will know it when you see it for it will look like an enormous dog grooming establishment. There will be dozens and dozens of grooming tables set up, all very close together. Almost every table will be occupied by a dog, attended by his handler or owner. The owner will be plucking, brushing, powdering, scissoring, or combing his pride and joy in a last minute effort to make him look better than every other dog in the ring.

A walk around this area can be a real eye-opener. You will see what a difference a simple steel comb can make in the texture of an already beautiful coat, how brushing the hair in a certain direction can make a dog look longer or shorter in body, and how a few hairs removed around the edges of a dog's ears can make him look so much neater.

The Concessions

In addition to the benching and grooming areas, there is often an area set aside at a show for concessions of various sorts. Take a walk through this area, too. You will find booths and counters where all sorts of dog-related products and services are offered for sale or simply for exhibit. There may

A groomer needs all the help he can get.

be dog books, buttons, dishes, leashes, food, t-shirts, patches, aprons, pictures, magazines, cages, grooming tools and all of the very latest novelty items for dogs. Some concessions will have free samples for you to take home with you. Others will have brochures or catalogs. Pick up some copies to take home, but don't start reading now because it's time to go into the ring area and watch the judging.

In the Ring

According to your catalog, the Old English Sheepdogs are being judged at 10:30 A.M. in Ring 3. Judging almost always begins on time, so at 10:15 sharp you must head for Ring 3. Out into the main ring area you go, to mix with the milling crowds, the dogs, and the cart-pulling members of the superintendent's crew once again.

Sometimes there are eight rings set up in the main arena; sometimes there are dozens of rings set up. There will be a sign on each ring telling what number it is. When you locate Ring 3, try to find a good place to stand because the single row of folding chairs around the outside of the ring will probably be occupied by the time you arrive.

Why not stay for the entire Old English Sheepdog judging and follow it in your catalog? Then ask yourself the following question:

Who Are Those People in the Ring Wearing Ribbons?

One of those be-ribboned persons in the ring is the judge. He will officiate over the entire Old English Sheepdog judging from beginning to end. The minute the proceedings begin, you will know which person is the judge. He or she will be giving directions and examining dogs. He will be the object of every handler's attention all the time. The Sheepdog judge for this show is Muriel K. DeCamp. Your catalog tells you that she is from Wisconsin and that she will later be judging German

Anne Palmer.

1978.

A good steward is necessary to keep things in order.

Shepherd Dogs and Alaskan Malamutes.

The other person in the ring is assisting her in various ways. This person is the steward. It is the steward's responsibility to make sure that the dogs and their handlers are in the ring when they are supposed to be there. He or she constantly checks the catalog to see that the numbers on the handlers' armbands in the ring correspond to the numbers in the catalog for a particular class. You see, the judge is not supposed to know the names of the dogs she is judging or the names of their owners. That's why numbers are used for identification. Usually it is the steward who hands out the armbands to the handlers and sees to it that any late comers make it to the ring in time for judging.

The steward assists the judge in other ways, helping to solve any problems that may arise, directing unsure handlers to stay in the ring or leave when their turn is over, and sometimes marking the winner's numbers on a chalk board for the benefit of the crowd. He or she also hands ribbons and prizes to the judge in the correct order, so his or her importance to the dog show is considerable.

The steward is usually a member of the club which is sponsoring the show. Although the position does not carry the recognition or the power of the judge's position, the steward contributes much to the show by making the judge's job easier. Without him, there would surely be mass confusion at several rings.

Classes for dogs? Sure, but not exactly like this one.

CHAPTER 6

CLASSES FOR DOGS?

Yes, show dogs go into their rings in classes. Like children in school, dogs are entered to compete against other dogs the same age, with roughly the same amount of show experience behind them. You will see each of these classes as you watch the Old English Sheepdog judging, and you will see why the class divisions are necessary.

If there are, let's say, twenty-seven Sheepdogs of all ages entered in this show, it would be difficult to judge all of them at once. That would be like taking kindergarten children, putting them in the same room with college students, and expecting them all to take the same test. To avoid this kind of inequity, our Sheepdogs, like the entries in every other breed, will be divided into different classes.

The first five classes are for dogs which are not yet champions. These classes are: Puppy, Novice, Bred by Exhibitor, American-bred and Open. One class is judged at a time, and blue ribbons are awarded to dogs and bitches that place first in each class.

After the five classes have been judged, and a winner selected from each, these five finalists will compete against each other for the title of Winners Dog or Winners Bitch. Then you will see the Specials—the champions of record—who will compete against one another and against the winner from the classes for Best of Breed.

Did You Say *Bitches*?

In the dog world, males are called *dogs*, and females are called *bitches*. The word *bitch* is used freely by dog show people. In fact, a person who says, "Is that a male or a female?" labels himself as an outsider with that question. An experienced "dog person" would say, "Is that a dog or a bitch?"

For those of us who have been trained from an early age not to use "that sort of language," the term *bitch* is likely to stick in our throats at first. We have to get used to it. After all, the first definition of the word in most dictionaries is "female dog."

In all of the classes, the dogs and bitches are judged separately in the interest of fairness. As with many other creatures, the male in the dog kingdom is likely to be larger and stronger than the female. Since it would be difficult for a dainty bitch to win over a huge, muscular dog, the sexes are judged separately, and ribbons are awarded to the best representative of each sex.

The Puppy Class

The judging has begun and into the ring come several charmingly clumsy, slightly undersized Sheepdogs. These are the entries in the Puppy Class. The class is open only to dogs under the age of eighteen months. A puppy must be at least six months old to qualify for entry.

You will notice that the puppies' behavior in the ring, while it is far from being outrageous is not quite as perfect and formal as that of the older dogs you will see later in the other classes. These Puppy Class entries are babies; they are given a certain margin of freedom that the older dogs will not need.

Recognizing the fact that a puppy changes greatly in his first year of life, the Puppy Class is broken down into three sections: puppies between six and nine months of age, puppies

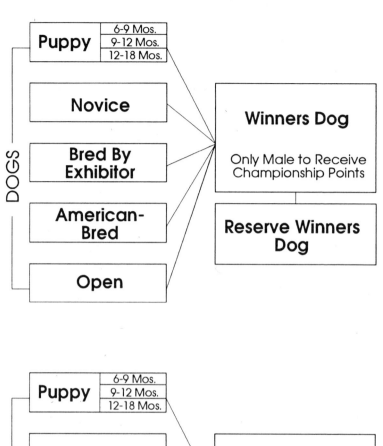

Succeeding in Show Business Chart

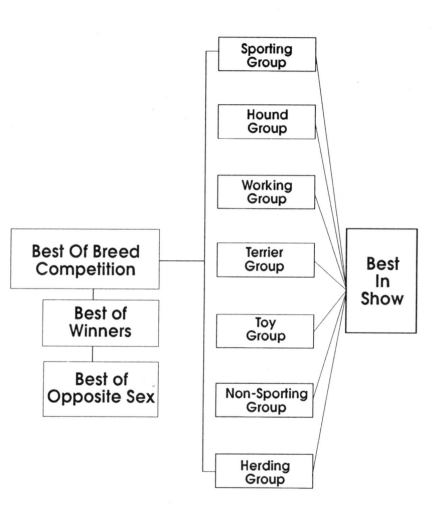

between nine and twelve months of age, and puppies between twelve and eighteen months of age.

It is possible for a Puppy Class entry to win his class and then go on later in the same show to win over older dogs and earn championship points. Many of the handlers in this class, however, have entered their puppies mainly to give them ring experience that will prepare them for competition in the other classes later on.

The Novice Class

The dictionary defines a novice as "one who is new to an activity; a beginner." This definition applies to the dogs entered in the Novice Class at a dog show.

In this class the entries are often young dogs with little or no ring experience. Some of them have been shown only in the Puppy Class. The Novice dog has not yet won three first-place ribbons in any class other than Puppy, and he has not won any championship points at all. In fact, if you have "show hopes" for your pet dog, this is the class in which you should enter him. Here you can see just how he compares with other fine dogs of his breed.

Some shows do not have Puppy or Novice Class competitions. One such show is the famous Westminster Dog Show, held every year in February at Madison Square Garden in New York City. For that very important event, every dog entered must have won a championship point to be eligible. If young dogs are pointed, they may be entered in the Westminster in the adult classes.

Many people who are new to the dog sport and are getting experience as handlers choose to show in the Novice Class because here they are not under the pressure of competing against the experienced handlers who show in the Open.

Bred by Exhibitor

When the entries in the Puppy and Novice Classes have been judged, and the winners in each have been given their blue ribbons, all dogs and handlers leave the ring. The next class, Bred by Exhibitor, enters the ring. In some breeds this is likely to be a small class, having perhaps only one or two entries. In the breeds that are very popular, however, this might be a very large class.

Bred by Exhibitor is open only to dogs which are shown by their breeders or by a close family member of the breeder.

American-bred

Dogs born in the United States as a result of a breeding that occurred in the United States may be entered in the American-bred Class. This is a good class in which to show an excellent dog that has outgrown the Puppy and Novice Classes, but which still does not have much ring experience.

As in all classes, the dog that wins receives a blue ribbon when the judging is completed, and then the entire class leaves the ring.

The Open

The Open is likely to be the largest of the five classes. It is called the Open for the obvious reasons: it is open to almost any member of the breed over six months old. Not too many young or inexperienced dogs compete in this class, though. Most of the Open entries are fairly mature, show-wise animals that may already have points toward their championships. In fact, many of the Sheepdogs that you see here probably are only a few points short of finishing.

It is interesting to watch these near-champions and to compare them to the Sheepdogs that you saw a few minutes ago in the Puppy and Novice. Not only are the Open dogs larger and more muscular, but they are also more sure of themselves and are likely to perform in the ring like real professionals. A blue ribbon goes to the winner of the Open.

More About Classes

The exact order of the breed judging is printed in your show catalog. In the classes, all of the dogs are judged together, and then all of the bitches are judged.

Dog show classes are a process of elimination that ultimately results in one entry being selected Best in Show. The first place in Dog and Bitch Classes are eligible to compete for Winners Dog and Winners Bitch. Each are then awarded points, determined by the number of dogs competing according to the AKC Point Schedule. The second-best dog or bitch is then chosen Reserve Winners, but receive no points.

Best of Breed consists of both male and female Champions plus Winners Dog and Winners Bitch. The Best of Breed award qualifies this dog to represent its breed in its Group. Best of Opposite Sex is then selected from the remaining dogs of the opposite sex to the Best of Breed.

First place winner in each of the seven groups represents its group for Best in Show.

If any one of these categories is missing from your catalog, it is for one of two possible reasons: first, there may not be such a class in that particular show (just as there is no Puppy Class at the Westminster), and second, it may just happen that no one chose to enter a dog in that class. In such a case, you might find two entries for Puppy dogs, followed by three entries in the American-bred Class, and then seven in the Open. This means that there were simply no dogs entered in Novice or Bred by Exhibitor.

Since you are watching the Sheepdog judging, you are quite likely to see all of the classes because this is a very popular breed. If you were to visit the ring in which Belgian Tervuren are being shown, you might find only two dogs—or even *one* dog—entered for the entire breed.

In each class the judge chooses the four best dogs and places them in order. After she has looked over every dog carefully and watched the manner in which each dog moves, she will line up all of the entries of a class together. She will take another long, scrutinizing look at them. Then she will quickly and forcefully point her finger four times—first, second, third, fourth—at the dogs she has chosen as the four best examples of the Sheepdog breed. Ribbons of different colors will be distributed to the handlers of the four dogs chosen, and all of the handlers will take their dogs out of the ring.

In each class it will be the holder of the blue ribbon who looks the happiest of all because for him the show is not yet over. In fact, for the winners of the five classes, the best is yet to come: Winners Class.

Winners Class

It is not possible to *enter* a dog in the Winners Class. The only way to get into this all-important judging is to win in one of the other classes.

When the dogs of all five classes have been judged, the first-place dog of each of those five classes is called back into the ring, each to compete against one another.

This is usually an exciting judging and an interesting one, for there will be some fine dogs in Winners. After all, every dog has already shown that he is better than all of the entries in his class. The excitement of the Winners Class results from the fact that this is the class in which championship points will be awarded.

When the Winners Class begins, the five dogs who placed first in Puppy, Novice, Bred by Exhibitor, American-bred, and Open Classes enter the ring together and are examined by the judge; she might spend less time with each dog now because she has already seen and evaluated them earlier. She knows these dogs.

The longer it takes the judge to make her decision, the more intense the atmosphere becomes in and around the ring. Everyone has a favorite by now and wants that favorite to take those precious points. By now, you must have decided on the Sheepdog that *you* would point to if you were the judge.

After what seems like an eternity, the judge turns, lifts her arm and points, lifts it again and points again. And, just like that, the deed is done. If you can't tell from where you're standing which dog she pointed to first, just look at the handlers to see which one is wearing the happiest smile. That's the handler of the Winners Dog, on his way to championship at last, if he's never been pointed before. If the dog already has points from other shows, maybe this win will put him over the top to championship.

The dog that the judge pointed to when she dropped her hand the second time is designated Reserve Winners Dog. This is the runner-up. He will receive no points unless the Winners Dog is, for some reason, disqualified by the AKC

The dogs of the Winners Class leave the ring at this point. Now it's the bitches' turn to vie for points. The same procedure is followed here. When the five classes of bitches have been judged, the winners of those classes enter the ring and are again examined. The judge's hand comes down two more times— Winners Bitch with championship points, followed by Reserve Winners Bitch. The other handlers usually congratulate the winning handler, you will see very little poor sportsmanship in the dog ring.

Those Precious Points

Points, points, points! That's all anyone seems to talk about around here. But how can you tell how *many* points these dogs have won?

For that information you must go back to that very helpful catalog. There will be a scale of points printed, usually in the front of the book. It lists the breeds entered at this show and, next to each breed, the number of points awarded to Winners Dog and Winners Bitch. Any win is valuable, even if it's only a one- or a two-point win. A win of three or more points is particularly important because it constitutes what is known as a "major." The number of points awarded is based on the number of dogs entered in a breed competition. More dogs mean more points.

To finish (in other words, to win his championship), a dog needs fifteen points under at least three different judges. Among these fifteen points must be two majors, each taken under a different judge. Thus, if a dog wins three 5-point majors at three different shows all under the same judge, he has fifteen points, but he is not a champion. Similarly, if a dog accumulates fifteen, or even twenty points from a long series of one- and two-point wins with no majors, he is not a champion either.

Here is an example of the manner in which a dog can become a champion:

Chicago show	Judge Morrow	4 points (major)
Fairville show	Judge Morrow	2 points
Detroit show	Judge Morrow	3 points (major)
Newton show	Judge Amato	1 point
Parkchester show	Judge Gleason	3 points (major)
Centralia show	Judge Sarris	2 points

Total 15 points

As you can see, this dog accumulated fifteen points under at least three (in this case, four) judges. At least two (in this case, three) of his wins were majors. Two of the three majors were won under different judges.

Anne Palmer.

The judge has just proven that you can't please everyone.

1978.

41

There is no time limit on finishing. We don't know if the dog in the example entered those six shows over a period of three weeks or six years, and it doesn't matter a bit.

There is also no limit on the number of shows in which a dog may be entered on his way to championship. Our dog might have entered only those six shows in which he earned points, or he might have entered a total of fifty or sixty shows of which he won only in six.

A champion is a champion, no matter how long it took him to finish.

What's a Ch?

Once championship has been achieved, the dog's name will be printed with the title "Ch." in front of it. Dear old Thunder will become Ch. Throgmorton's Foggybottom of Thunder Hill, and sweet little Cupcake will be listed as Ch. Judy-Mae's Peppermint Cupcake Cutie Pie.

The American Kennel Club keeps a record of all championship points awarded at all shows. When a dog earns his championship, the AKC checks his record thoroughly.

CHAPTER 7

THE STARS of the SHOW

As you watched the judging of the Sheepdogs, you might have noticed that the crowd gradually grew thicker around the ring as the judge progressed toward the Open. Winners Class probably drew quite a large group of new spectators. Now that the classes are over, the crowd develops into a throng. Many more people have joined you. Why? They want to see the stars of the Old English Sheepdog world, the dogs which are already champions and are competing for Best of Breed. This group of dogs is known as the "specials." Now you're in the Big Time.

Boys and Girls Together

The specials differ from the earlier judging in that dogs and bitches enter the ring together. In Best of Breed competitions the two sexes vie directly with one another.

Anne Palmer.   1978.

Step aside, Miss America, here comes a real winner!

You will notice a distinct difference between the dogs now in the ring and those you saw earlier in the classes. These champion dogs probably have had much ring experience. Since they are all seasoned winners, they probably seem to enjoy participating in the show. There will be a considerable amount of strutting and prancing here. Most of these dogs are used to their handlers as a result of having performed under them many times. This also adds to the polished appearance of their performances.

The only dogs in the Best of Breed competition that are not already champions will be two that you already know—the Winners Dog and Winners Bitch that you cheered for in the Winners Class a few minutes earlier.

Although no championship points are given for winning Best of Breed, this win carries much prestige. Some really fine dogs have won hundreds of Best of Breed ribbons.

Best of Winners

An offshoot of the Best of Breed competition is the judging known as Best of Winners. There are only two entries—Winners Dog and Winners Bitch—old friends of yours by now.

The judge looks once more at the two Winners and chooses the one that she thinks is the better of the two. This is Best of Winners. This win may or may not carry extra points.

Let's say that in the Sheepdog competition, the Winners Dog took five points because there was a huge entry of dogs. The Winners Bitch, however, earned only three points because there were fewer bitches entered in the classes. Now the judge decides to award Best of Winners to the bitch. The bitch now picks up two extra points because she has beaten a dog that has won two points more than she has. The Winners Dog gets to keep his five points, and the Winners Bitch also gets five points for going Best of Winners over him.

Best of Opposite Sex

The winner in Best of Opposite Sex may be either a dog or a bitch. When the Best of Breed winner is a bitch, the judge will take another look at the dogs and choose the best of them as Best of Opposite Sex. If the Best of Breed winner, on the other hand, is a dog, she chooses the finest bitch entered as Best of Opposite Sex.

At this point the dog show is over for all of the Sheepdogs except one, the Best of Breed winner. He or she will participate in the Group competition, which will take place after all of the breeds have been judged. All of the other Sheepdogs will go back to their benches if this is a benched show. If the show is unbenched, the handlers and their dogs may stay to watch other judgings, or they may go home to recover from the excitement of the day.

"I don't care what anyone says. I think he's extremely handsome."

CHAPTER 8

SOMETHING FOR EVERYONE

Now that you have watched a breed judging from beginning to end, what can you do to fill the hours between now and the Group judging at the end of the day?

Why not walk to various rings and look at some of the more than 135 breeds of dogs recognized by the American Kennel Club? See how many of the breeds you recognize. If a breed is unfamiliar, don't be afraid to ask someone at ringside what it is.

You cannot help noticing the wonderful variety that exists in the world of dogs. A person looking for a hairy giant will find several different breeds to suit his taste, and so will the individual who longs for a good-natured dog that is so ugly that it breaks the heart of some to look at him, for in the Bulldog breed, ugliness is beauty.

You will find dogs in all sizes and colors, with every kind of coat length and texture. Each dog was originally bred to help his human owner in some way, and it is according to this original purpose that the AKC still categorizes dogs by distinct groups.

Dog Groups

There are seven groups in American dogdom. They are the Sporting Dogs, Hounds, Working Dogs, Terriers, Toys, Non-Sporting Dogs, and Herding Dogs. At some shows there

"What are you laughing at? He's a sensational watch dog—
trained to kill on command!"

49

will be another group of dogs known as the Miscellaneous Class. This consists of breeds that are not yet recognized by the AKC, such as the Border Collie, but which do exist as separate breeds and which may be working toward recognition. Although they sometimes appear in a special class at shows, they cannot win points, nor can they compete in Group judging.

The seven recognized groups, as we pointed out are organized according to the function they perform, or did perform in the past, for the benefit of their owners.

The Sporting Group

Sporting Dogs are those dogs that were bred to assist their masters in the sport of hunting. There are various types of pointers who will literally point—stretching forward until their bodies become living arrows— at a bird which the hunter, with his merely human senses, cannot see or hear. This group also includes the setters—Irish, English, and Gordon—and the spaniels, which flush birds from their cover.

Because these dogs are meant to go into the field and hunt for long hours with their masters, most of them are strong dogs of a good size, and many of them have short flat coats. These coats afford enough protection from twigs and brambles, but are not so long as to become matted or otherwise damaged by work in the field. Every dog in the group was bred to point, flush game, or retrieve game. The five types of retrievers all have the soft mouth needed to bring a bird in without breaking bones, skin, or feathers.

In spite of their history as field dogs, the sporting dogs are a fine-looking lot. They are shown in the traditional "stacked" position, in which the legs, head, and tail are placed by the handler so that the dogs look like living statues—heads up, necks stretched forward, tails out straight, back legs straining to show perfect angulation—motionless and elegant.

1978.

Anne Palmer.

**The Sporting Group includes setters (Gordon, top), pointers
(Weimaraner), and Spaniels (English Springer and Cocker.)**

51

1978.   Anna Palmer.

**The Hound Group includes, among others, the Afghan (top),
Coonhound, Norwegian Elkhound, Whippet, and Beagle.**

SPORTING DOGS

Pointer, Brittany
Pointer, German Shorthaired
Pointer, German Wirehaired
Retriever, Chesapeake Bay
Retriever, Curly-Coated
Retriever, Flat-Coated
Retriever, Golden
Retriever, Labrador
Setter, English
Setter, Gordon
Setter, Irish
Spaniel, American Water

Spaniel, Clumber
Spaniel, Cocker
Spaniel, English Cocker
Spaniel, English Springer
Spaniel, Field
Spaniel, Irish Water
Spaniel, Sussex
Spaniel, Welsh Springer
Vizsla
Weimaraner
Wirehaired Pointing Griffon

The Hound Group

Hounds are also hunting dogs, but unlike the Sporting dogs, they chase the game, sometimes into a tree or a hole, and keep it there at bay, barking continuously until the hunter arrives on the scene.

This group is made up of twenty different hound breeds, including several that have become very popular as pets, such as the Afghan Hound, the Dachshund, the Beagle, the Saluki and the Norwegian Elkhound.

There are two kinds of hounds: scent hounds and sight hounds. The scent hounds, as the name suggests, hunt with their noses, sniffing the ground and shrubbery for the scent of the prey. Most scent hounds—like the Beagle, Basset, Coonhound, Bloodhound, and Dachshund—have long, floppy ears. These ears, it is believed, serve them well in their work, acting as fans to wave the scent from the trail toward the dog's nose as they flop back and forth along the trail.

Sight hounds, as you can guess, hunt by sight rather than scent. They are generally rather tall dogs, like the Greyhound and Irish Wolfhound, and, because they don't need long, floppy ears, they don't have them!

What a sight hound does need is speed. Some of these dogs are among the fastest animals on earth. Greyhounds and Whippets are used as racing dogs. Borzois—once known as Russian Wolfhounds—are extremely fleet dogs.

Although most hounds are lean ("Skinny as a hound dog," as the old saying goes), there are a few very stocky hound breeds that were developed to work with large game. Rhodesian Ridgebacks were used years ago in Africa by lion hunters, and Norwegian Elkhounds really hunted elk.

HOUNDS

Afghan Hound	Harrier
Basenji	Ibizan Hound
Basset Hound	Irish Wolfhound
Beagle	Norwegian Elkhound
Black and Tan Coonhound	Otter Hound
Bloodhound	Petit Bassett Griffon Vendeen
Borzoi	Pharaoh Hounds
Dachshund	Rhodesian Ridgeback
Foxhound, American	Salukis
Foxhound, English	Scottish Deerhound
Greyhound	Whippet

Working Dogs

The Working Group is large and varied. It consists of dogs that have done all kinds of work for their masters. Most were herding dogs, sled dogs, or guards of one sort or another.

In the Working Group, you will find many dogs who have become great favorites with the American public, like the ubiquitous German Shepherd Dog.

You would expect dogs who work for a living to be large in size, and most of them are: the Great Dane, Great Pyrenees, Saint Bernard and Mastiff are all in this Group.

WORKING DOGS

Akita
Alaskan Malamute
Bernese Mountain Dog
Boxer
Bullmastiff
Doberman Pinscher
Giant Schnauzer
Great Dane
Great Pyrenees
Komondor

Kuvasz
Mastiff
Newfoundland
Portugese Water Dog
Rottweiler
Saint Bernard
Samoyed
Siberian Husky
Standard Schnauzer

The Working Group includes the Great Dane (top), Saint Bernard, Rottweiler, and Siberian Husky

The Terrier Group

The Latin word *terra* means *earth*. Terriers were meant to "go to earth," or dig in the ground, after rats, badgers, and other small animals. Because this is dangerous work, terriers are usually brave and feisty animals. Visit any terrier ring and you might hear a bit more barking than you hear elsewhere. If two terriers pass one another without at least a short series of challenging barks, it is unusual, for they are a cocky lot and love to show that they are not afraid of anything.

The terriers that will be most familiar to the show visitor are probably the Scottish Terrier (Scottie), the West Highland White Terrier (Westie), and the Miniature Schnauzer, all of which have become very popular as pets.

TERRIERS

Airdale Terrier
American Staffordshire Terrier
Australian Terrier
Bedlington Terrier
Border Terrier
Bull Terrier
Cairn Terrier
Dandie Dinmont Terrier
Fox Terrier, Smooth
Fox Terrier, Wire
Irish Terrier
Kerry Blue Terrier

Lakeland Terrier
Manchester Terrier
Miniature Bull Terrier
Miniature Schnauzer
Norfolk Terrier
Norwich Terrier
Scottish Terrier
Sealyham Terrier
Skye Terrier
Soft-Coated Wheaten Terrier
Staffordshire Bull Terrier
Welsh Terrier
West Highland White Terrier

78.

Anne Palmer.

The Terrier Group includes the Airedale (far left), the Welsh Terrier, Bull Terrier and Miniature Schnauzer among its 25 members. The Airdale is one of the largest.

57

1978.

Anne Palmer.

Among the members of the Toy Group are (left to right) the Yorkshire Terrier, Brussels Griffon, Toy Poodle, Pug, and Papillon.

58

The Toy Group

The Toy Group was assembled more on the basis of size than of function. All members of this group are, of course, very small, but that's about the only thing they have in common. Some of them, like the Chihuahua, have never done any kind of work as far as we know. Others—the Pekingese, for example—existed in very early times mostly as status symbols for wealthy and powerful people, to be given as gifts to important visitors and to serve as household companions and pets.

These small dogs have long served humans in that very important capacity, the household companion and pet. The toy breeds already mentioned are very numerous in this country and abroad. Other toy favorites are the Yorkshire Terrier, or Yorkie, the Pomeranian, the Toy Poodle, the Shih Tzu, and the Maltese.

TOYS

Affenpinscher	Miniature Pinscher
Brussels Griffon	Papillon
Chihuahua	Pekingese
Chinese Crested	Pomeranian
English Toy Spaniel	Poodle (Toy)
Italian Greyhound	Pug
Japanese Chin	Shih Tzu
Maltese	Silky Terrier
Manchester Terrier (Toy)	Yorkshire Terrier

The Non-Sporting Group

This group is a rather strange combination of dogs that seem to have nothing at all in common with one another except the fact that none of them fit neatly into any of the other groups.

Some great favorites from this group that have caught the public fancy are the Bichon Frise, Boston Terrier, Dalmatian, Bulldog, Lhasa Apso, and the Miniature and Standard Poodles.

Certain dogs from the Non-sporting Group undoubtedly performed some kind of work in the distant past. The original Poodles, for instance, were once water retrievers. However, the functions performed by these dogs are so far in the past that they are all but forgotten. Today the members of this group exist—like the toys—mainly to provide friendship for their owners.

Other lesser known members of the Non-sporting group are Chow Chows, French Bulldogs, Keeshond, Schipperkes, and Tibetan Terriers.

NON-SPORTING DOGS

Bichon Frise	Keeshond
Boston Terrier	Lhasa Apso
Bulldog	Poodle
Chow Chow	Schipperke
Chinese Shar-Pei	Shiba Inu
Dalmatian	Tibetan Spaniel
Finnish Spitz	Tibetan Terrier
French Bulldog	

Herding Dogs

The Herding Group was created from dogs that were formerly working dogs, they were bred to herd cattle and sheep. They range in size from very large, to the Welsh Corgis, whose low-to-the-ground bodies enable them to nip at the heels of the livestock they were bred to herd. They are equally as good with herding children and make wonderful family pets.

The Non-sporting Group. Four of its members are the French Bulldog (left), the Tibetan Terrier, the Keeshond, and the Dalmatian.

61

HERDING DOGS

Australian Cattle Dog

Bearded Collie

Belgian Malinois

Belgian Sheepdog

Belgian Tervuren

Bouvier des Flandres

Briard

Collie

German Shepherd Dog

Old English Sheepdog

Puli

Shetland Sheepdog

Welsh Corgi, Cardigan

Welsh Corgi, Pembroke

Miscellaneous Class

In this class are dogs that may compete in conformation shows but will not be awarded any points toward their championships and may only compete in obedience trials and to win the appropriate obedience titles.

This class is not just for any breed not officially recognized by the American Kennel Club, but only those breeds in which the AKC has determined a strong interest is shown and a substantial amount of breeding activity has taken place over a wide geographic area. If the growth of the breed is healthy and its numbers steadily increase in the miscellaneous class, then it can be admitted for registration in the AKC stud book and compete in regular conformational classes.

MISCELLANEOUS CLASS

American Eskimo

Australian Kelpie

Australian Shepherd

Border Collie

Canaan Dog

Cavalier King Charles Spaniel

Greater Swiss Mountain Dog

Spinoni Italiani

Which Shall I Watch?

With more than 135 breeds to choose from, how do you decide which rings to visit? The best answer to this question is: "Go with your fancy." Walk around a bit. If the dogs being judged in Ring 6 appeal to you, stay there awhile. Or, if you

**Among the Herding Group are the Bouvier des Flandres (top),
German Shepherd Dog, Old English Sheepdog, Smooth Collie,
and the Welsh Corgi Cardigan.**

see a lone Pug trundling along with her handler toward another ring, and if this Pug flirts with you, follow along. Maybe you'll see a new friend go to Best of Breed.

The most important thing now is for you to enjoy yourself. Don't try to learn all of the breeds in one day. Don't try to memorize all of the judging rules today either. Just have a good time. There will be many more shows in your future.

Anyway, what with the breed judgings, the concessions, the benching area, and the grooming area to visit, you won't be lacking for things to do between now and the Group competition.

Among the Miscellaneous Class are the Greater Swiss Mountain Dog, Spinoni Italiani, and the Canaan Dog.

Winners of the seven group judgings will compete for Best in Show. Which one will take home the silver?

1977.

Anne Palmer

Stacking her dog (rear view).

CHAPTER 9

THE MAKING OF A SHOW DOG

✩A Star Is Born✩

The dogs that you see on those benches and in the rings were bred by specialists in their particular breed or variety. A top-winning dog often comes from a long line of winners.

Beauty, good bone structure, a fine coat, superb color and markings, perfect health, acceptable temperament—these are the qualities that a show dog must have. And they are inherited qualities, for the most part. They do not happen by accident. Therefore, if Joey Duncan, your next-door neighbor, breeds his skimpy-coated Collie to his brother's skimpy-coated Collie, then Joey cannot expect a litter of profusely-coated Collies to be the result of the breeding.

A show winner is usually the result of long experience in a breed and of careful planning. A breeder who has owned Poodles for several years, attended shows, has learned everything he can about hereditary traits in Poodles, and has access to a dog and a bitch that he believes to be compatible, may consider breeding the two. Usually he will do so only if he believes that the resulting puppies will be as good as, or better than, their sire and dam.

True show dog breeders are not producing puppies for profit. They are interested in producing only a small number of champions, not in supplying dogs in quantity to sell to the public.

For most people in the sport of dogs, breeding, raising, and showing dogs is a hobby—sometimes a rather expensive one. They earn their livings at other jobs: they are teachers, bus drivers, mechanics, writers, actors, doctors, nurses, police officers, and members of almost every profession on earth.

When these people bring a puppy into this world, you can be sure that it will have a good chance of becoming a star!

☆ How Do I Know If My Skippy's A Star ☆

Let's suppose that Toby Thompson has a Scottish Terrier that's going on two years of age. He acquired the dog from a reputable breeder of show-quality Scotties, and Toby thinks that Skippy is the most beautiful dog that ever lived in this world. Maybe he is, and if so, there is a way to find out.

The Standard

For every breed recognized by the AKC there is a written description called the Standard. If Toby wants to know whether Skippy really is the most beautiful Scottie in the world, he should obtain a copy of this standard from the AKC (51 Madison Avenue, New York, NY 10010) or from one of the many excellent dog books available in book stores.

The Scottie Standard, like most of the Standards for other breeds, is a detailed explanation of what a Scottie is expected to be. It is broken down into sections with headings such as "Skull, Muzzle, Eyes, Coat, Color," etc. Each section tells the Scottie owner what to look for in that area. For example, here is the section on eyes:

Eyes (5 points)—Set wide apart, small and of almond shape, not round. Color to be dark brown or nearly black. To be bright, piercing and set well under the brow.

The Scottie Standard, like those of many other breeds, contains a section called "Penalties." This tells you those points which are considered very undesirable in a breed. This is the Penalties section for the Scottie Standard:

Penalties—Soft coat, round or very light eye, overshot or undershot jaw, obviously oversize or undersize, shyness, timidity or failure to show with head and tail up are faults to be penalized. No judge should put to Winners or Best of Breed any Scottish Terrier not showing real Terrier character in the ring.

So you see that the Standard describes not only what the dog should look like, but also, in many cases, how the dog should act and what kind of character or personality he should have.

If Toby Thompson goes through the Scottie Standard, sentence by sentence, finding that his beloved Skippy conforms to every characteristic of the Standard, then Toby knows that Skippy really is a potential star.

It is these breed Standards that show judges use when they choose their winners in the ring. The judge of German Shepherd Dogs does not say. "Well, Number 7 here, is cuter and fuzzier than Number 8, so I'll give Number 7 the ribbon." That's just not the way dogs are judged. Instead, the judge thinks more along these lines: "Number 7 certainly is cute and fuzzy, but the Standard for this breed calls for the dogs' coats to be dense and harsh, so I can't give him the ribbon. Number 8 on the other hand, has a dense, harsh coat. He also has the "direct and fearless expression" called for in the standard. The ribbon will go to Number 8."

Dogs are not judged by comparing them to one another; they are judged by comparing each individual dog to the standard for its breed.

That's A No-No

All of the dogs that you see at any show will be purebred dogs, but not every purebred dog is allowed to enter a show. There are certain disqualifying traits that make a dog of any breed ineligible for entry in shows.

A blind dog, for example, may not be entered in a dog show. Show dogs must be "sound," or normal, in all ways.

Blindness indicates a physical abnormality and thus disqualifies the dog from entry in a show. Other automatic disqualifications apply to deafness, lameness, monorchidism and cryptorchidism (conditions in which one or both testicles do not descend from the scrotum of a dog).

A dog which has been spayed or castrated is also disqualified. Part of the reason for holding dog shows is to improve the quality of the breeds. Since a spayed or castrated dog cannot be used in a breeding program and can in no way contribute to the improvement of the breed, there is no point in showing such a dog in conformation shows.

The final disqualification results from any attempt to change the dog's appearance by artificial means. No artificial hair coloring, for example, can be used to improve the color of a dog's coat. Dew claws may be surgically removed on most breeds, and ears may be cropped in such breeds as the Great Dane and Doberman. Tail docking is also acceptable in breeds where it is traditional, such as Boxers, Poodles, and Old English Sheepdogs.

☆ Coaching the Star ☆

Lucky Toby Thompson has himself a star Scottie, or so he believes and hopes. Now he must get that potential star ready for his show debut. This means coaching, or training Skippy for long hours.

The owner of a show dog naturally wants his dog to make a good and lasting impression on the judge. That means that in addition to beauty and character, the dog must have good ring manners. He must learn how to stand correctly and to stand still for examination, so Toby must pose Skippy and gently hold him in the correct show pose until Skippy learns to stand still on command. Skippy must also learn to allow strangers to touch him, run their hands over him, and look at his teeth.

Toby must work with Skippy on the nylon leash known as a "show lead," so that Skippy will be able to walk in any direction at any speed and will automatically assume the show pose when he comes to a stop.

All show dogs must be taught to go into and out of cages and to travel in them because all show dogs eventually have to spend some time in a cage, either at a show or on the way to one.

Skippy must learn to be a good traveler for he will be going to many out-of-town shows. Most dogs like to ride in cars, it seems, so this shouldn't be a problem for Toby.

The dogs that you see at a show have been trained for stardom almost from the day they were born. Toby is at a disadvantage because he didn't even think of showing his dog until Skippy was almost two years old. It can still be done, though, and with hard work and lots of patience, Toby and Skippy may just go all the way to the finish—championship!

☆ Making the Star More Beautiful ☆

You already know that much of the beauty of the show dog is the result of his breeding. No amount of grooming can turn an ordinary house pet into a Best in Show winner, just as no amount of make-up can turn the boy next door into Tom Cruise.

Proper grooming can, however, make a superb dog stand out from other dogs in the ring. You must have seen a number of different grooming procedures during your visit to the grooming area.

Grooming procedures, of course, vary with different breeds. Most breeds are simply cleaned and brushed with very little trimming needed. Doberman Pinschers, for example, are simply given a bath, if they need one, a few days before the show. The toenails are kept short, and the hair is cleaned out of their ears and footpads. Any stray long hairs may be plucked or scissored from the ears, feet, or tail, and their coats may be polished with a chamois, a piece of velvet, or a hound glove.

Terrier breeds, on the other hand, sometimes need a great deal of meticulous grooming. Some of the terriers are hand-plucked or stripped. This means that, instead of being clipped with electric clippers, the dog's coats are pulled out by hand or with a tool when the dog is shedding. It gives the coat the desirable harsh or wire-like texture, and it allows the coat to retain a pure color.

The breed that most of us think of first when the subject turns to grooming is the Poodle. This is a breed for which grooming is of prime importance. If you visit a Poodle judging, you will see that all of the entries are sporting variations of the traditional "Lion Clip," which they must wear to qualify for entry. The two most common types of Lion Clip seen in American shows are the Continental, in which the rear end of the dog is clipped clean with only two pompons at the hips, and the English Saddle clip, in which a short pack of hair remains on the dog's hindquarters.

These Poodle clips take great skill and lots of time to execute. A good many of the dogs that you see in any grooming area will be Poodles.

The long-haired breeds like the Lhasa Apso, Shih Tzu, Old English Sheepdog, and Afghan Hound also need careful grooming. Most of the work with such breeds is brushing and combing, but some trimming is also usually done. This is partly to emphasize a dog's good points or de-emphasize his not-so-good points. For example, a little judicious trimming in the right places can make a tail look longer or shorter. Brushing in a certain direction can emphasize the angulation of the rear legs or the shortness of the dog's back.

No artificial means may be used, however, to change a show dog's appearance. Those apricot-colored Poodles you see at shows are really orange in color. They were born that way and received no assistance from hair dyes. Similarly, the owner of a Dalmatian with too few spots is not allowed to help Mother Nature along by adding a few more spots with black grooming chalk or shoe polish.

Every Star Has His Own Manager

Movie stars, rock stars, and even many sports stars have their own agents or managers who book appearances for them, arrange for hotel accommodations, handle money arrangements, and generally smooth their way. Dog stars are no different. A dog can't enter himself in a show and then parade around the ring alone, accepting his winner's ribbon by grabbing it with his teeth. This is one star who really needs a manager, and that manager will be a handler, owner, or owner-handler.

Handlers, Owners and Owner-Handlers

These are three separate and somewhat confusing terms. Let's take them one by one:

Handler: A handler is the person who is at the human end of the leash while the dog is in the ring.

Owner: The owner is the person whose name is thus listed on the dog's AKC registration papers.

Owner-Handler: The owner-handler is one who owns the dog and who also takes the dog into the ring and shows him.

Then what is a *professional* handler? Okay, a professional handler is a person who handles other people's dogs and is paid for doing so. Usually the professional handler is a person who has had a great amount of experience with dogs. If Toby Thompson wanted Skippy to enter a big dog show but was too timid to go into the ring himself, he might hire a professional handler to show Skippy for him.

Handlers have different arrangements with the owners whose dogs they show. Sometimes the handler keeps the dog with him all or nearly all of the time. In other cases, the owner

Not everyone can handle certain breeds.

might just meet the handler at each show and give his dog to the handler for just the amount of time it takes the handler to present the dog in the ring.

A professional handler, with his wealth of knowledge and experience, can sometimes get a dog to perform better than the dog's owner who just doesn't have the know-how to set the dog up in such a manner that a judge will notice all of the dog's good points. In such a case, owners might prefer to hire a professional handler to show their dogs—either at every show in which the dogs are entered or in the most important shows such as the ones in which the wins are majors.

Some professional handlers have dozens of clients. You will see these handlers arriving at the dog shows in buses and trucks. They will unload crates and tables and boxes and chairs and all kinds of equipment. Some such handlers bring fifty or more dogs to one show. They might even have a small army of assistants who travel with them, helping with the packing, grooming, and ring work.

Other professional handlers might prefer to handle only a few dogs. With some of these people, handling is more of a weekend hobby than a means of earning a living.

Getting the Show on the Road

If you think that it's hard to pack for yourself when you're going away for a weekend, just imagine what the show dog owner goes through when he prepares to set out for a show. He must have a crate for his dog. He also needs a collapsible grooming table on which to brush and trim his charge. He must take along food and water for his dog, as well as dishes to put them in. Although water is always available at a dog show, many owners don't like to take the chance of their dogs getting sick on water that they're not used to.

The owner will also have to take all of the brushes, combs, scissors, clippers, and other grooming supplies he will need for

Anne Palmer.

Professional handlers arrive with a *few* of their show dogs.

BILL AND JAN BIGWIN
PROFESSIONAL HANDLERS
ALL BREEDS

1978.

those last minute touch-ups.

If it is an outdoor show, equipment must be packed to help the dog and owner deal with whatever kind of weather transpires.

That could mean raincoats, boots, and umbrellas, heavy coats and extra blankets, or bags of ice cubes in insulated buckets for very hot days.

Most owners take along some sandwiches for themselves because the food offered at refreshment stands at dogs shows might not be all that is desired.

How to Succeed in the Dog Show Business

All of the good breeding and grooming and careful preparation and training in the world cannot make a star out of a dog that doesn't want to be a star.

The perfectly proportioned Scottie who is unhappy in the role of star will show with his ears down, and the judge won't look at him twice. That handsome Alaskan Malamute, if he doesn't like to show, may spend his whole time in the ring whining softly. He won't be looked at, either.

The true star will be the dog who loves to show—the "showing fool." This is the alert and snappy little show-off who just can't wait to get into that ring, eyes bright, ears and tail up, dying to make those other dogs look second rate, seeming to know somehow that he's a star.

CHAPTER 10

THE GROUP JUDGING

By the time all of the breeds have been judged, it is late afternoon or early evening. Now the real drama of the show begins with the Group competitions.

Re-Grouping

The rings in which the breeds were judged are taken away by the superintendent's crew. For the Group judgings, the entire floor of the arena will be used. At an outdoor show, a very large area will be roped off for the competition. People will pull up chairs around this area or will simply sit on the grass to watch.

The seven groups are always judged in the same order: Sporting, Hound, Working, Terrier, Toy, Non-sporting, and Herding. The dogs competing in Group are the ones that won Best of Breed earlier in the day.

Good Judgment

A person who judges a Group must have a special license from the AKC to do so. In order to obtain this license, the person must prove that he or she is thoroughly familiar with the Standards for all of the breeds in the Group. In other words, if there are more than twenty breeds in a Group, as there are in Sporting, the judge must know all the Standards. The same is true for judges of the other six Groups.

During the Group judging, the judge will carefully examine each entry and will have his handler gait him around the ring. This means that he will ask the handler to take the dog around the ring at a trot or a fast walk in order to show that the dog moves properly for his particular breed.

"Take Them 'Round, Please!"

When all of the Group entries have been examined and gaited individually, the judge will send them all around together, usually with the well-known show command: "Take them 'round, please!"

At this point, the spectators nearly always react with spontaneous applause and cheers: the sight of twenty or more fine champions, all Best of Breed winners, gaiting around that ring together is enough to bring even a casual spectator to his feet.

When dogs and handlers are again at their places, the judge may call forward a number of dogs for a second look and may ask some of them to "go 'round" once more for another look at the movement.

Winning Ways

Now it is time to choose the winners. After a few moments of silence that seem to last forever, the judge's hand rises and falls four times just as it did in the breed judging. First, second, third, and fourth place have been bestowed on those four dogs who, in this judge's opinion, come closest to being perfect examples of their breeds.

The other six Groups are judged in the same manner. In the Toy Group, however, and for some breeds in the Terrier and Non-Sporting Groups, the small dogs are examined on a table set up at one end of the ring. This is simply because it is very hard on a judge to have to get down on his knees to examine very tiny dogs. Except for this difference, Group competitions are all the same.

When the Groups have all been judged, you will begin to sense an atmosphere of growing suspense in the crowd, for the climactic moment, toward which this whole day has been headed, has at last arrived.

Judging small breeds on a table saves wear and tear on the judge's back.

The sterling silver trophy awarded to the Best In Show winner at the Westminster Dog Show.

CHAPTER 11

BEST IN SHOW

The moment that everyone has waited for has finally arrived. The electrified atmosphere is somewhat comparable to the excitement created in the last inning of a closely-contested World Series between two evenly-matched baseball teams.

Now *one* and *only one* of the seven dogs that placed first in the Groups will be chosen as Best in Show, the highest honor that a show dog can attain.

The gleaming silver trophy sits majestically on a table in plain view, waiting to be awarded to the winner. The Best in Show judge now makes his appearance. At the larger shows, the Best in Show judge usually does not officiate at any of the preliminary events. If the judge is a woman, she will be wearing a formal gown. A male judge will be attired in a tuxedo. This particular judge is one who has exceptional qualifications: he is specially licensed to choose this winner. This judge has demonstrated his ability to judge *all* of the breeds recognized by the American Kennel Club; not just members of a particular Group, but all the dogs from the seven Groups.

The chosen few handlers who have made it to this part of the show have managed to conceal their weariness. They are usually dog show veterans, since it would be practically impossible for a handler to win a Group on his very first attempt. Even though these seven handlers are veterans, their pulses quicken and their hearts race as the end draws near.

The ring is cleared and the contenders enter in Group order to much applause from the appreciative spectators. Let's say that we have a fine, handsome Irish Setter from the Sporting Group, a stately Borzoi from Hound, an heroic Saint Bernard from Working, a feisty Scotty from Terrier, an elegant silver Poodle from Toy, an imposing red Chow from Non-Sporting, and our good friend the Old English Sheepdog from the Herding Group.

The customary ring procedure is again followed. The judge examines each dog carefully, not revealing his opinions by any word, gesture, or facial expression. He then sends all seven dogs around the ring a few times with their handlers. The judge will look the dogs over individually at some length, examining them with his hands, searching for some fault or some outstanding quality, and then—while the crowd holds its breath—he dramatically points to the winner. This time the judge only points once, for there is no runner-up to Best in Show.

Our friend the Sheepdog has made it all the way to the top! He is the one who will take home the silver, and you have had the thrill of watching a "showing fool" go from the breed judging all the way to Best in Show.

To the cheers and applause of the crowd, the judge hands the Best in Show trophy to the Sheepdog's handler. Congratulations are shouted, flash bulbs pop all around as photographs are taken, the handlers kiss, hug, and shake hands with each other as the winner's friends rush to join him in the ring amid the excitement, and the show has come to an end.

I sincerely hope you have enjoyed yourself, and I hope that you will have the pleasure of attending many more dog shows.

Picking a winner isn't easy!

Junior handling: An important feature of dog shows.

86

CHAPTER 12

SOMETHING FOR THE YOUNG

There is something for everyone at a dog show. Every age group is represented including the very young.

Junior Showmanship is for boys and girls between the ages of 10 and 17. This category was set up to develop the talents of young people who later may become top show handlers or even judges.

In Junior Showmanship, it is the handler who is judged, not the dog.

For girls and boys who are 10, 11, and 12 years of age, there is Novice Junior Showmanship. Novice Senior is for handlers between the ages of 13 and 17. Both of these classes are for handlers who have not won a first place in any of the Novice divisions. If a young person has won a first place at a "points show," then that person is eligible to compete at the Westminster Dog Show at Madison Square Garden in New York City the following February.

From the ranks of Junior Showmanship come many of the serious exhibitors of tomorrow.

21st Annual Dog Show Poster 1897

CHAPTER 13

DOG SHOWS OF THE PAST

The history of dog shows is a surprisingly tumultuous one, marked by scandal, confusion, heated disagreements, and finally, order and dignity.

It was during the nineteenth century that dog shows, as we now know them, first were held. The very earliest shows "happened" without any formal planning, when proud dog owners gathered in local parks, clubs, and taverns to show their dogs off to one another.

These same proud owners formed the first kennel clubs, partly to protect, establish, and promote their breeds, and partly for the good fellowship the clubs provided.

Pugs of All Nations

One very early show was open only to toy dogs. It was organized by Davenport Bromley in England and was held the 30th of May in 1850. It boasted "Pugs of All Nations" and was attended by the cream of English society. The proceeds went to charity, and Bromley was able to use his considerable influence to persuade many titled persons to exhibit their dogs. This event undoubtedly helped to popularize the sport of dog shows in England since *everyone* wanted to do what the Beautiful People do, then as now.

One Jemmy Shaw founded a club for toy dog owners, also in England. The shows staged by this club were more like today's carnivals than they were like today's dog shows. They advertised and delivered "rat-killing terriers." The most famous of these little marvels was a Toy Manchester Terrier known as Tiny the Wonder. Tiny weighed 5 1/2 pounds and once killed 200 rats in just three hours, clearly distinguishing himself as an early champion of sorts.

Most of the Terrier breeds were originally bred to search out rats and other similar pests.

Anne Palmer. 1978.

In the nineteenth century, bull baiting and other blood sports which had enjoyed great popularity with the public were abolished by an act of Parliament. This paved the way for dog shows, which caught the public attention. The era of the wonderful spectacle had begun.

Show Biz for English Dogs

The lush green splendor of Hyde Park in London was the setting in 1851 for the first Great Exhibition. There were no prizes or ribbons. This was simply an opportunity for the people of London to stroll through the park on a fine day and observe the various types of dogs on exhibit there.

A few years later the first organized dog show was held. It is recorded in the English Kennel Club Stud Book, 1859-1874. The entry read as follows:

1859—the first dog show ever held, organized by Messrs. Shorthose and Pape, at the suggestion of Mr. Brailsford, in the town hall of Newcastle upon Tyne, on the 28th, and 29th of June, 1859. There were 60 entries.

Two classes of dogs, pointers and setters, were represented at the 1859 show. The victor in the pointer group was

a dog named Lord Derby which—it just so happened—
belonged to one of the judges. Naturally, the dog chosen as the
best setter, one Dandy, belonged to the other judge!

The public didn't seem to mind the hanky-panky, however. They were clamoring for more of these delightful events.
Thus, more and more shows were held, and eventually breed
clubs became more numerous.

In 1873 the Kennel Club of Great Britain was formed. It
was responsible for bringing a certain order to the dog sport.
A stud book was established, and rules were made and
enforced. This took time, of course, but over the years the sport
of dogs became a very respectable one indeed throughout all
of England.

Back in the Colonies

Dog shows were probably held informally throughout the
United States from the middle of the nineteenth century. The
earliest recorded show, however, was held in Chicago in 1874.
Although there were many entries, no awards or prizes were

given. That same year a show was held in Oswego, New York, and only one dog was entered! Eventually, however, the idea began to catch on. Shows were held, many dogs were exhibited, and prizes and awards were handed out. All of this was done with great enthusiasm, but in a rather haphazard manner, in many different cities and villages.

courtesy of AKC Gazette 1924

New York, N.Y.

Meanwhile in New York City, a group of dog fanciers met at the Westminster Hotel at Irving Place and East 16th Street. This small but enthusiastic group decided to hold the First Annual New York Bench Show for Dogs. This group was, of course, the Westminster Dog Club, and the show that they held was the first Westminster Dog Show.

The show took place at Gilmore Gardens at Madison Avenue and 26th Street in May of 1877. Originally planned as a one-day event, this show generated so much interest that it was extended an extra day. There were 1,201 dogs exhibited at the show before a panel of five judges. The catalog was a staggering 73 pages long. With thirty-four different breeds represented, this was by far the most spectacular exhibit ever held in America up until that time.

The first Westminster show received much attention from the newspapers of the day, which heralded it as an enormous success. From that day to this, the Westminster has far outshone any other dog show in this country.

Westminster—The Nobel Prize of the Dog World

For a dog to win Best in Show in *any* dog show is a tremendous honor, but to go Best in Show at Westminster is truly the dog owner's fondest dream.

The Westminster Dog Show has been held every year since 1877 and is the second-oldest regularly-held sporting event in the United States. (The Kentucky Derby is the oldest.) The Westminster is still a two-day show and it is now, as it has always been, a benched show. Although it is far from the largest show in this country, the Westminster is the most prestigious.

The American Kennel Club

The American Kennel Club, or the AKC as it is usually called, was formed in 1884, also in New York City. It is second

only to the Lawn Tennis Association as the oldest amateur sports governing body in this country.

One of the first aims of the AKC was to set up a code of regulations to govern dog shows. Another aim was to publish a reliable stud book for use as a breeding reference. The AKC itself has no individual members but is made up; of various dog clubs.

Today the AKC Stud Book contains the names of more than 15 million purebred dogs with more than a million being added annually. The AKC publishes a monthly magazine called *Purebred Dogs: The AKC Gazette*. It also issues and approves the breed Standards by which all dogs are judged. And it was the AKC that supervised the development of the point system by which today's dogs finish their championships.

Today the AKC occupies offices at the corner of Madison Avenue and 26th Street, in New York City, very close to the exact spot where the first Westminster Dog Show took place over one hundred years ago. The AKC has approximately 500 member clubs, 2,300 licensed clubs, and houses one of the finest dog libraries in the world. It also has a superb collection of dog paintings and prints, as well as a huge file of photographs.

CHAPTER 14

GIFTED DOGS—THE WORLD OF OBEDIENCE

So far we have talked only about the conformation shows in which dogs are judged against their breed Standards with little or no regard for their intelligence. What about the dog who is extremely intelligent and well-trained? He deserves a chance to show off too, and in the Obedience Trial he is given this chance.

To enter an Obedience Trial, a dog does not have to conform perfectly to his breed Standard. As long as he is an AKC-registered, purebred dog, he may have the wrong kind of ears or legs, he may be an unacceptable color, or he might be over or undersized. He can be altered or spayed, or he can be well beyond the age at which dogs are considered to be beautiful.

In the world of obedience, it's brains that count, not beauty, but that doesn't mean that you will see a bunch of doddering old uglies here either. Many dogs who are entered in Obedience Trials have already earned their championships in the conformation ring. Some dogs work toward conformation and obedience titles at the same time.

Obedience Trials

An Obedience Trial is exactly what its name denotes: a show (trial) in which dogs are judged on their ability to obey the commands of their handlers.

Some Obedience Trials are held at conformation shows. Usually the obedience rings are at one end of the arena, more or less separated from the conformation rings.

At outdoor shows where there is a great deal of space available, you might have to hike across an open field to find the obedience rings, but *do find them* because the obedience dogs put on a very good show indeed.

Obedience-trained dogs do not do tricks, however, so don't be disappointed when they fail to roll over and play dead or walk on tightropes. The exercises that these dogs have learned are practical ones that make them better able to fit into the lives of their owners.

There are several different levels of obedience and for each level at which a dog proves that he can perform satisfactorily, he is granted an obedience title which will be used after his name, just as the Ch. title in conformation is used before his name.

C.D.—The Novice Class

The first title in obedience is the C.D.—Companion Dog. To earn a C.D. a dog and his handler must prove in three separate trials that together they can perform six exercises to the satisfaction of three different judges. The exercises in the Novice Class are: heel on lead, stand for examination by judge, heel off lead, long sit (sitting for several minutes), long down (lying down for several minutes) and recall (returning to handler when called).

Judges score the obedience competitors on a scale of zero to 200 points. A score of 170 points or higher gives a dog a "leg" toward his title. This means that he wins one of the three steps toward C.D. He must score above 170 points in two more "legs"—to earn the right to carry the C.D. title after his name. When he does this, he will be known as Curry's Thunder, C.D., or Strutter of Wakefield, C.D.

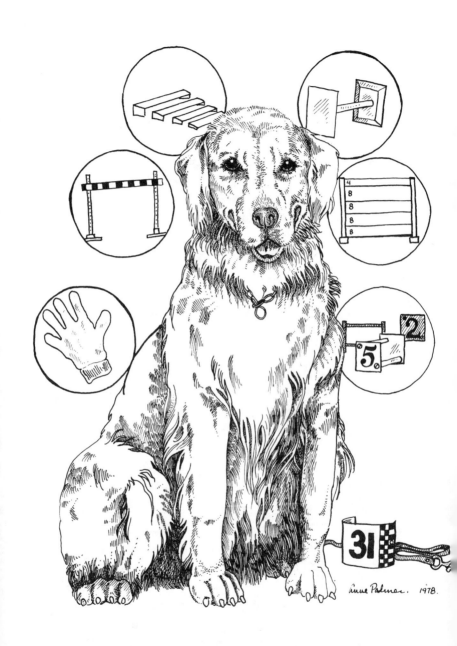

Obedience trials!

If the dog also has his championship in conformation, he now becomes Ch. Curry's Thunder, C.D., or Ch. Strutter of Wakefield, C.D.

C.D.X.—Open Obedience

After a dog wins his C.D., his owner might decide to train him for the Open Obedience Class, in which he will try to earn his C.D.X. (Companion Dog Excellent) title.

This class, as you would expect, involves more complicated exercises. Here the dog must jump over obstacles (a broad jump and a high jump) and retrieve a thrown glove and a dumbbell.

In Open Obedience the dog will be placed on a Long Down by his handler. The handler will then leave the ring and walk to a place where his dog cannot see him. After several minutes the handler will return, but during the time he is out of the ring, the dog must remain down, without moving from the place where his handler left him.

If a dog can get through these difficult exercises, among others, in three different trials, he earns his C.D.X.

U.D. and U.D.T.—Field Trials

A rare dog might be very gifted and lucky enough to have an owner who knows how to train him properly. This dog could go on to great heights in Obedience. He might succeed in the directed retrieving, jumping, and scent discrimination that lead to the U.D. (Utility Dog) title.

Beyond the U.D., he could be trained to follow a scent. This could lead to competition in Field Trials in which dogs are expected to "track," or to follow a scent in the field. These trials lead to the U.D.T. (Utility Dog, Tracking) title.

Field Trials differ for different breeds and are designed to test the dog in the kind of work he was originally expected to do. Thus, retrievers are tested on their ability to retrieve, or

1978.

Anne Palmer.

At a field trial, a retriever does what he was born to do.

fetch, the birds shot by their handlers, both on land and in water.

Hounds are tested on their skill in chasing rabbits, while pointers are expected to freeze in the pointing position when they sense the presence of a game bird. Spaniels look for birds in the underbrush and, when they find them, chase them into flight. This is called "flushing the game," and it is on their ability to flush game that spaniels are judged.

Superdog!

There is a new "Superdog" title now. It is the O.T.Ch. (Obedience Trial Champion) for dogs who have earned all of the obedience titles and are able to go on to more and more complicated exercises. These dogs compete in special trials with other very advanced obedience-trained dogs. Only a few dogs have won this title, which, unlike the other obedience titles, is carried before, not after, the dog's name. One well-known Superdog is O.T.Ch. Tonka, a Golden Retriever that has given near flawless performances in obedience trial competition.

Commonly Used Abbreviations

In the dog fancy, those who exhibit their pedigreed charges continually have occasion to use the same terms over and over again which indicate different levels of winning. Because these terms are rather lengthy, frequently when they are written they fall into natural abbreviations known to the knowledgeable exhibitor. Below is a list of those abbreviations.

SBIS: Specialty Best In Show
BIS: Best In Show (All Breeds)
BOB: Best Of Breed
BOS: Best Of Opposite Sex
BOW: Best Of Winners
RWD: Reserve Winners Dog
RWB: Reserve Winners Bitch
WD: Winners Dog
WB: Winners Bitch

Dog Show Listing

Listed below are the names of some of the largest kennel club shows held annually in the United States. These represent only a portion of the shows held as there are hundreds of dog fanciers all over the country that have banded together to form clubs to promote their mutual interests in their particular breeds. Many of these clubs are qualified to sponsor dog shows of varying sizes. The following list, however, does not represent the national specialty shows wherein all the entries must be members of only one particular breed. (These specialty shows are very important in establishing the worth of a particular specimen within his breed.) And it cannot indicate all of the smaller specialties held in conjunction with the larger all-breed shows, which is a usual practice. But it does give an indication of the activity to be found for the interested show dog exhibitor and point out a direction in which to start. These shows offer a wealth of information and instruction, for they not only demonstrate how top dog shows are organized and run but also offer some of the finest specimens in dogdom for those new to the fancy to see how the standards of the various breeds are actually embodied.

Consult the AKC Gazette for a complete up to date listing.

ASHEVILLE KC
Swannahoa, NC

ATLANTA KC
Alpharetta, GA

BALTIMORE COUNTY KC
Timonium, MD

KC OF BEVERLY HILLS
Los Angeles, CA

BOARDWALK KC
Atlantic City, NJ

BUCKS COUNTY KC
Erwinna, PA

CENTRAL OHIO KC
Columbus, OH

CLEARWATER KC
Tampa, FL

DETROIT KC
Detroit, MI

DEVON DOG SHOW ASSC.
Ludwigs Corner, PA

EVANSVILLE KC
Louisville, KY

FORT WORTH KC
Fort Worth, TX

GOLDEN GATE KC
Daly City, CA

HARRISBURG KC
Harrisburg, PA

HOOSIER KC
Indianapolis, IN

HOUSTON KC
Houston, TX

INTERNATIONAL KC
Chicago, IL

KERN COUNTY KC
Bakersfield, CA

LANCASTER KC
Lancaster, PA

LEAVENWORTH KC
Kansas City, MO

LOUISVILLE KC
Louisville, KY

MARYLAND KC
Baltimore, MD

MENSONA KC
Santa Rosa, CA

OLD DOMINION KC
Centerville, VA

OLD DOMINION KC
of N. VIRGINIA
Reston, VA

ORANGE EMPIRE DC
San Bernadino, CA

OXRIDGE KC
Stamford, CT

KC of PHILADELPHIA, PA
Philadelphia, PA

RAVENNA KC
Ravenna, OH

SACRAMENTO KC
Sacramento, CA

SAHUARO STATE KC
Phoenix, AZ

SANTA ANNA VALLEY KC
Cypress, CA

SANTA BARBARA KC
Buellton, CA

SANTA CLARA VALLEY KC
San Jose, CA

SANTA CRUZ KC
Santa Cruz, CA

SCOTTSDALE DFA
Scottsdale, AZ

SEQUOIA KC
Tulare, CA

SILVER BAY KC
Del Mar, CA

SIR FRANCIS DRAKE KC
San Rafael, CA

SOUTH WINDSOR KC
Springfield, MA

SUN MAID KC of FRESNO
Fresno, CA

SUPERSTITION KC
Mesa, AZ

TAMPA BAY KC
Tampa, FL

Texas KC
Dallas, TX

TRENTON KC
West Windsor Township, NJ

VENTURA COUNTY DFA
Ventura, CA

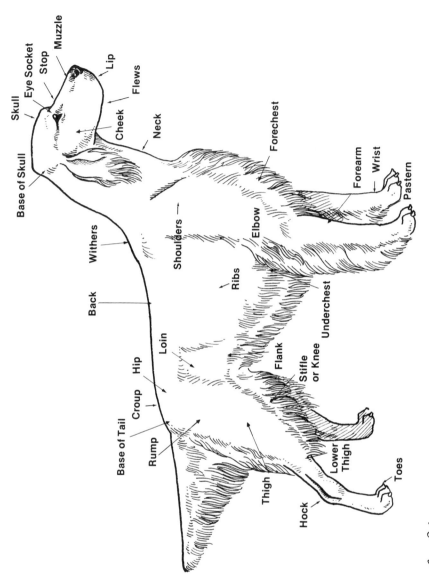

1979.

Anna Palmer.

Canine Anatomy

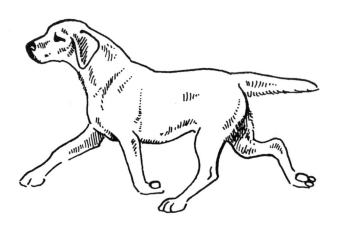

Good Movement/Poor Movement (side views)

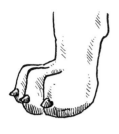

Cat Foot

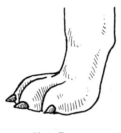

Hare Foot

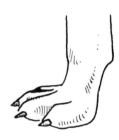

Paper Foot

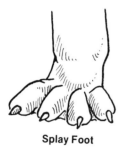

Splay Foot

Anne Palmer. 1979.

Dog Feet

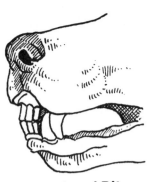

Level Bite

Overshot Bite

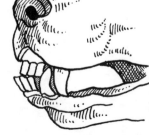

Undershot Bite

Dog Bites

Anne Palmer.   1979.

108

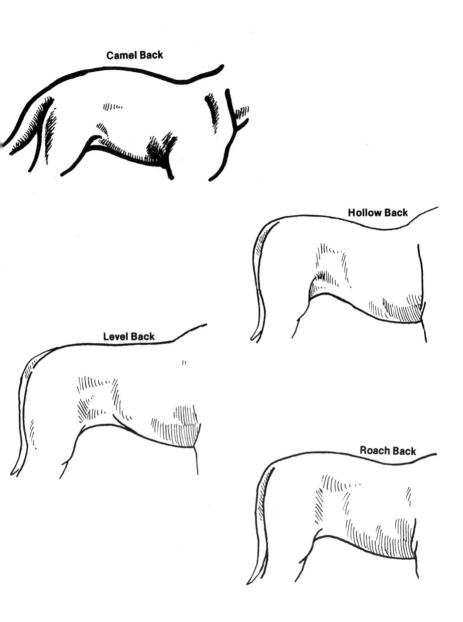

Camel Back

Hollow Back

Level Back

Roach Back

Dog Backs

Froggy

Cheeky

**Broken Up
Face**

Dog Faces

Dish Faced

Down Faced

Roman Nose

Apple Head

Domed Head

Wedge-shaped Head

Snipey Skull

Bumpy Skull

Dog Heads

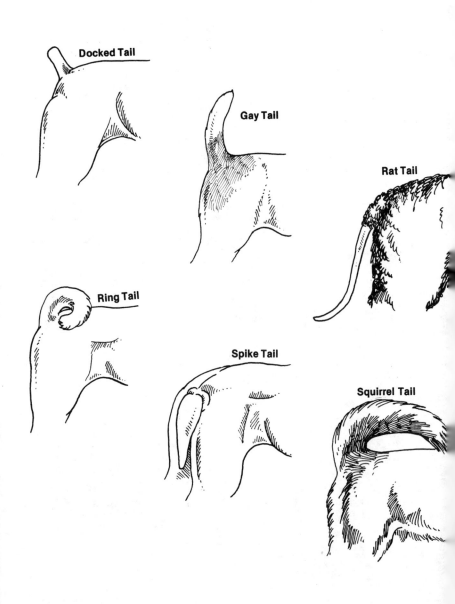

Docked Tail

Gay Tail

Rat Tail

Ring Tail

Spike Tail

Squirrel Tail

Dog Tails

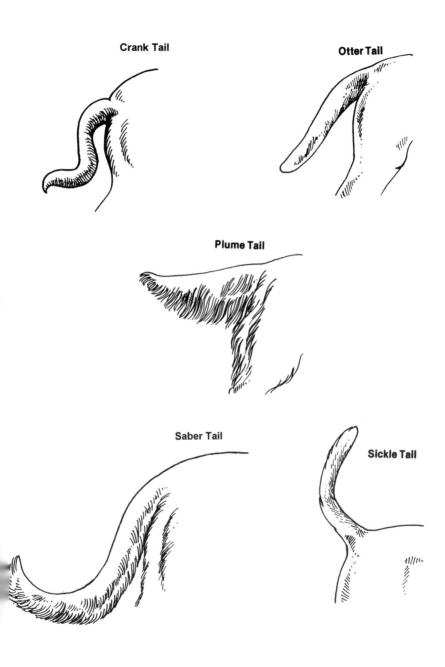

Crank Tail

Otter Tail

Plume Tail

Saber Tail

Sickle Tail

Dog Tails Continued

113

Button Ear

Prick Ear

Semi-prick

Cropped Ear

Rose Ear

Bat Ear

Hanging Ear

Anna Palmer.

1978.

Dog Ears

DOG SHOW GLOSSARY

Action: The way the dog moves (walks or trots).

Almond eye: Having oval-shaped eyes.

Angulation: The angles formed by the joints of the dog's body, particularly the legs.

Apple head: Rounded skull.

Apron: A mass of thick, long hair on the dog's chest.

Arm band: A numbered band worn by exhibitors at a dog show as a means of identification.

ASCOB: Any Solid Color Other than Black, a variety of the Cocker Spaniel.

Back: Area of a dog's back between shoulders and base of tail.

Bad mouth: A mouth in which the teeth are crooked, undershot, or overshot.

Bait: Tidbit, usually liver, used to keep a dog attentive in the ring.

Balance: Having all parts of the body in proper proportion to one another.

Barrel ribs: Well rounded ribs.

Bat ear: An upstanding ear that faces front and is quite large in proportion to the size of the dog's head, as in the French Bulldog.

Beefy: Overly muscular or heavy.

Belton: A coat color in which white hair is mixed with blue, lemon, or orange, as in the English Setter.

Benching area: Area at a show in which dogs are exhibited on benches.

Bitch: Female dog.

Bitchy dog: A male dog that has a feminine appearance.

Bite: The way the upper and lower teeth meet each other.

Blaze: A stripe of light color on the fore part of the head.

Blocky: Having a heavy, squared-off head.

Bloom: Good coat condition.

Blown coat: A coat that is shedding, as in "He blew his coat."

Blue merle: Bluish marbling in coat, as seen in Collies, Shelties.

Bobtail: Having no tail, as in the Old English Sheepdog.

Bossy: Too muscular in the shoulder area.

Brace: Two dogs of the same breed shown as a pair.

Bracelets: Round puffs of longer hair on the legs of a Poodle.

Breeching: Lighter coloring on insides of back legs.

Brindle: A marbling of black hairs in a coat of tan, brown, or gray.

Brisket: That part of a dog's body between the two front legs.

Burr: The pinkish area inside a dog's ear.

Butterfly nose: A nose with both dark and light pigment.

Buttocks: The dog's rump.

Button ear: Ear that folds forward, as in the Fox Terrier.

Camel back: A back which curves upward in the middle.

Canines: The long, pointed teeth on the upper and lower jaw of the dog, just behind the incisors (front teeth).

Cat foot: A foot that is round with toes held tightly together.

Chalking: Changing or enhancing the color of a dog's coat with chalk or any similar substance.

Champion: A dog that has won 15 points in conformation competition under three different judges. The points must include two major wins. The abbreviation *Ch.* appears before the name of a champion dog.

Character: The dog's "personality."

Cheeky: Having puffy cheeks (sides of the face).

Chest: Front of dog below the neck and above the front legs.

China eye: Blue eye.

Chiseled: Having fine, clear lines.

Chops: Heavy skin on lower jaw, as in the Bulldog.

Clip: The way a dog, particularly a Poodle, is trimmed, as in the puppy clip or the Continental clip.

Cloddy: Heavy in appearance or movement.

Close coupled: Having a relatively short back.

Close in back (Close behind): Moving with the back legs too close together.

Coarse: Having thick, unrefined features.

Cobby: Short and compact in body.

Collar: White or light-colored band of hair around neck.

Conformation: The physical structure of a dog, particularly as it conforms, or matches up to the Standard.

Conformation Show: A dog show in which dogs are judged according to how well they measure up to the breed Standard.

Coupling: The area between the last rib and the hip bone.

Cow-hocked: Having back feet that turn outward and hocks that turn inward.

Crabbing: Moving with the body on a slant so that the back legs are to the left or right of the front legs.

Crated: Confined in a crate or cage.

Crest: The arched part of the back of the neck.

Cropped ears: Ears that have been surgically trimmed so that they are short and upright, as in the Doberman Pinscher.

116

Croup: That part of a dog's back that is directly above the hips.

Crown: The top of the head.

Cryptorchid: Lacking properly placed testicles. This is a disqualification in all breeds.

Culote: Long, fluffy hair on the backs of the rear legs.

Dam: A dog's mother.

Daylight: As "There's too much daylight under this dog," refers to excessive length of leg.

Dewclaws: Claws appearing too high up on the legs to be useful. In many breeds, dewclaws are removed during puppyhood.

Dewlap: Fold of skin on throat, as in Bloodhounds.

Dish-faced: Having a concave line to the muzzle between eyes and nose.

Disqualification: A serious fault in conformation, such as a white coat in a German Shepherd Dog, which makes a dog ineligible to compete in a conformation show.

Distemper teeth: Teeth that have been marked or yellowed by the disease known as distemper.

Docked tail: A tail surgically cut to a certain length.

Dog: A male dog, as opposed to a bitch. Any dog when discussing dogs in general.

Doggy bitch: A female dog that has a masculine appearance.

Dog fancier: A person who is interested in dogs and dog shows.

Domed head: A high and rounded skull, as in the Bloodhound.

Double handling: A method of keeping a dog on its toes in the ring by having someone outside the ring distract him.

Down-faced: Having a muzzle that slopes severely downward.

Down on pasterns: Having weak ankle joints so that legs bend too far backwards at ankles.

Drive: Strong movement, especially in the hindquarters.

Drop ear: Ear that hangs flat against the head, as in the Poodle.

Dry neck: A neck on which the skin is tight to the muscle, as in the Whippet.

Dudley nose: Flesh-colored or liver-colored nose.

Ear fringes: Long hair on the edges of the ears.

Elbow: The joint between the forearm and the upper arm.

Entry: A dog that is entered in a show.

Even bite: Teeth that meet with no overlapping.

Ewe-necked: Having a concave neck.

Exhibitor: The person who enters his dog in a show.

Expression: General appearance of the head and, particularly, the eyes.

Fall: A thick mass of hair covering the stop and muzzle, as in the Kerry Blue Terrier.

Fault: A physical or mental imperfection, such as shyness in Scottish Terriers or yellow eyes in Airedales.

Fawn: Light brown, tan.

Feathering: Long hair on legs, tail, or ears, in spaniels and setters, especially.

Feisty: Peppery in temperament, quarrelsome. This is a desirable characteristic in some breeds, such as the Scottish Terrier.

Fiddle faced: Having a long, excessively narrow face.

Fiddle front: Bowlegged in front with feet turning outward.

Fill: Excessive skin or muscle below the eyes.

Finish: To go to championship.

Flag: Long, tapered feathering on the tail, as in setters.

Flank: The lower part of the dog's back.

Flat-sided: Not having properly rounded ribs.

Flews: Loose skin on the lips.

Flicking pasterns: Loose movement of the lower part of the front legs.

Forearm: That part of the front leg between the elbow and pastern (ankle).

Foreface: That part of the head from just in front of the eyes down to the nose.

French front: See *Fiddle front.*

Frill: Long hair on a dog's chest.

Fringes: See *Feathering.*

Front: The front legs, chest, brisket, and shoulders.

Full eye: Round eye.

Fun match: A match held for practice and enjoyment.

Gaiting: Moving, as in fast walking or trotting.

Gay tail: A tail carried high over the back.

Gazehound: See *Sighthound*

Grizzle: A coat in which white hair is mixed with the darker main color of the coat.

Hackney: A type of gait in which the front legs move higher than they should.

Handler: The person who shows a dog in the ring and who may or may not be that dog's owner.

Hare foot: A long, narrow foot.

Harlequin: White with black markings, as in some Great Danes.

Harsh coat: Wire-haired or stiff coat.

Haw: Membrane inside the lower eyelid.

118

Height: In dogs, height is measured from withers to ground.

High stationed: Tall and long-legged.

Hip Dysplasia: An abnormal hip formation which causes lameness.

Hock: The visible joint on the rear leg above the ankle. Prominent in the German Shepherd Dog.

Hound ears: Long, hanging ears, as in the Beagle.

Hound-marked: White with brown and black markings, as in the Basset Hound.

Huckle bones: Top part of the hip bones.

Jacket: The tight coat on the body of a terrier.

Jowls: Heavy skin on the lower jaw.

Kinked tail: A tail that is noticeably bent.

Knuckled over: Having legs that bend outward at the pasterns (ankles).

Layback of shoulder: The angle of the shoulder blades.

Leather: The skin of the ear.

Leggy: Having long legs.

Level bite: See *Even bite* .

Loaded shoulders: Overly muscular shoulders.

Loose lead: A lead (leash) that is held loosely so that the dog moves naturally, without undue lifting or pulling.

Loose movement: An uncontrolled gait.

Major: A show win carrying three or more points.

Mane: Long, thick hair around the neck.

Mantle: A "cape" of darker hair over the back.

Mask: Lighter or darker mask-like marking on the face, as in the Siberian Husky.

Merle: See *Blue Merle.*

Miscellaneous Class: A class in a dog show for breeds that are not yet recognized by the American Kennel Club.

Monorchid: Having only one properly placed testicle; a disqualification in all breeds.

Obedience Trial: A dog show in which dogs are judged on their ability to obey the commands of their handlers.

Occiput: The upper point of the skull.

Otter tail: A tail that tapers from thick at the root to narrow at the tip.

Out at elbows: Having elbows that are not properly close to the body.

Overshot: Having upper teeth that protrude over the lower teeth.

Pacing: An undesirable type of movement. When a dog paces, his two right legs move forward while both his left legs move backward.

This pattern is repeated, giving the dog's movement a rocking appearance.

Paddling: A gait in which the dog's front feet swing too far out to the sides.

Parti-color: A coat containing two or more colors. Characteristic of such breeds as the Old English Sheepdog, but a disqualification in others, such as the Poodle.

Pastern: The "ankle" of the dog.

Penciling: Lines of black hair on face or legs.

Pigeon-toed: Having toes that turn inward toward one another.

Pile: Undercoat.

Pincer bite: See *Even bite*.

Pointed: Having earned one or more championship points.

Points: Areas of color on muzzle, feet, ears, and tail.

Poking: Moving with the head carried too low and too far forward.

Pompon: A rounded tuft of hair, as on the tail of a clipped Poodle.

Premium List: Official announcement of a dog show, sent to show dog owners ahead of time. It contains such information as date, location, and names of judges.

Prick Ears: Ears that stand up straight naturally, as in the Silky Terrier.

Pull the stick: Ask for a dog to be measured officially.

Punishing jaws: Strong, powerful jaws.

Put down: Conditioned and groomed, as in, "That Poodle is beautifully put down." Also, not chosen or placed by the judge, as in, "That judge always puts my dog down."

Put up: To choose a winner, as in, "I hope he puts up that Collie."

Quit: To stop performing before the judging is complete.

Racy: Long in the leg and slender in body.

Rangy: Long in body.

Rat tail: A hairless, tapering tail, as on the Bedlington Terrier.

Reach of front: Having a strong, lengthy, front leg movement.

Ring tail: Tail carried in a curl over the back.

Roach: High, curved area of lower back, as in the Bedlington Terrier.

Roan: A mixture of white and colored hair.

Roman nose: A muzzle which curves upward from the nose to the forehead.

Rose ear: A small ear which folds back in such a way that the inside of the ear is visible, as in the Bulldog.

Ruff: See *Mane*.

Running sheet: The schedule of judging.

Saber tail: Tail that is carried low behind the dog and that curves slightly upward.

Sable: Mixture of black hair over a light coat, as in some Collies.

Saddle: Pattern of color or texture over a dog's back in the shape of a saddle, as in the Afghan Hound.

Scent hound: A dog that hunts by scenting its prey, as does the Beagle.

Scissors bite: A mouth in which upper teeth slightly overlap the lower teeth.

Screw Tail: Short, spiral-shaped tail.

Set up: Position the dog to stand correctly for the judge.

Shown free: Handled on a loose lead.

Sickle tail: Tail carried up and outward in a half circle.

Sidewinding: See *Crabbing*.

Sighthound: A hound that hunts by sight, as the Saluki.

Sire: A dog's father.

Slab-sided: Having flat sides, lacking rounded rib cage.

Slew foot: Foot that turns outward.

Snipey: Having a muzzle that is too pointed.

Sound: Physically and mentally normal.

Sparring: Letting two dogs, usually terriers, face each other to determine their courage.

Spayed: Surgically altered to prevent pregnancy.

Special: A dog, usually a champion, that is entered in the Best of Breed judging. ("I specialed him," means that the owner entered his dog in the Best of Breed competition.)

Spectacles: Dark markings around the eyes, resembling eye-glasses, as in the Keeshond.

Spike tail: Tail resembling a carrot.

Spring of ribs: Roundness of the rib cage.

Square: Measuring the same from withers to rump as from withers to ground.

Stacked: Posed for examination.

Standard: A written description of the physical and temperamental characteristics of a certain breed.

Steward: A person who assists the judge in the ring.

Stifle: The "knee" part of the rear leg.

Stilted: Choppy in movement.

Stop: Recessed area between the eyes, characteristic of most breeds but not present in Collies and Bull Terriers.

Straight in hocks: Having fairly straight rear legs, as in the Chow Chow.

Straight in pastern: Having straight ankles.

Stripping: Grooming, especially of terriers, by removing hair from coat.

Strung up: Held high on a very tight lead.

Substance: Sufficient bone and muscle.

Superintendent: A person who organizes, sets up, and supervises a dog show.

Team: Four dogs of the same breed shown together.

Throaty: Having loose skin hanging on the throat

Thumb marks: Black spots on the backs of the legs near the feet.

Ticking: Dark hair mixed into a white, or very light, coat.

Timber: Bone.

Topline: The line of the dog's back from withers to tail.

Trace: Line of dark hair running down the back.

Tricolor: White, black, and tan.

Tuck up: A "thin waist," as in Greyhounds.

Type: Conformation to Standard.

Typey: Having all necessary characteristics of a breed.

Undershot: Having lower teeth that extend forward beyond upper teeth.

Walleye: Eye of a very light color.

Weedy: Having delicate bone.

Well let down: Having good angulation in rear legs.

Wet neck: Having loose skin in neck area.

Wheaten: Tan, the color of wheat.

Wire-haired: Having a wire-like coat, as in Airedale Terriers.

Withers: High point of the back directly above the front legs.

Wry mouth: A mouth in which the lower jaw is to the right or left of the upper jaw.